# Mikoyan
# MiG-21

# Mikoyan
# MiG-21

## Bill Gunston

Published in 1986 by Osprey Publishing Limited
27A Floral Street, London WC2E 9DP
Member company of the George Philip Group
© Bill Gunston 1986

Sole distributors for the USA

Osceola, Wisconsin 54020, USA

British Library Cataloguing in Publication Data

Gunston, Bill
    Mikoyan MiG-21.—(Osprey air combat)
    1. MiG (Fighter planes)
    I. Title
    623.74'63    UG1242.F5

    ISBN 0-85045-734-3
    ISBN 0-85045-652-5 Pbk

Editor Dennis Baldry
Designed by Gwyn Lewis
Filmset in Great Britain by Tameside Filmsetting
Limited, Ashton-under-Lyne, Lancashire, and printed
by BAS Printers Limited, Over Wallop, Hampshire

FRONT COVER
*A MiG-21MF interceptor of the East German Air Force
(Luftstreitkrafte und Luftverteidigung, LSK) gets
airborne with a.t.o. rockets burning*

TITLE PAGES
*Flanked by a MiG-17, this MiG-21PFS is on display
at the Soviet Museum of the Armed Forces. The same
aircraft is seen again on page 79*

# Contents

# Introduction

This book is about the most famous fighter in the world. To many who read this book this will seem to be a provocative statement. Others will consider it nonsense.

What do we mean by fame? Some dictionaries merely equate the word with renown, and then to define renown bring back the word fame. Most suggest that fame means not just notoriety but good, or generally approved, notoriety. Can we really apply this word to the MiG-21, which to most of us in the West is the arch bad guy?

Let's stand back a bit, maybe take a small terrestrial globe in our hand, and reflect for a moment that the Western world is not the same as the world. To be a fighter you do not have to have a number with a capital F prefix. To be a fighter pilot you do not have to wear a NATO uniform. To fly a MiG-21 does not automatically make a pilot an evil aggressor. Indeed, one's opinion of what constitutes an aggressor depends sharply on one's viewpoint. One man's 'terrorist' is another man's 'freedom fighter', both views being sincerely held.

The author would much prefer to leave such political semantics entirely out of a book about an aeroplane. This is hard to do. Most other books in the Osprey Air Combat series have introductions written from what might be called a 'far Western' viewpoint. The good guys are 100 per cent good, the bad ones wholly bad. To read the other volumes in this series one would conclude that the only good MiG is a dead one.

This book was not written just to redress what had certainly became an imbalance. The reason why most publishers produce books is to make money. A book that tried to set the record straight, or give the other side's viewpoint, but which was unlikely to find buyers, would be unlikely to find a publisher. The MiG-21, however, rates a book in this series on just about every count one can imagine.

It has been built in more versions than any other fighter since World War 2.

It has been built in greater numbers than any other fighter since World War 2.

It has had the longest active life of any combat aircraft in history, and is certain to go on for a long while yet.

It has been involved in more wars in more diverse parts of the world than any other fighter in history.

It has equipped more air forces than any other fighter in history; the current assessments range from 'at least 37' up to '49', numbers which no Western fighter can approach.

It is this last factor which makes the MiG-21 the 'most famous' fighter. The basic Madison Avenue approach is a straightforward count of heads, and on this basis the MiG wins hands-down. There is little point in guessing at even the roundest of numbers, but for every human who has heard of the F-15 (for example) there must be three who have heard of the MiG. In terms of population rankings, the MiG-21 is used by countries 1, 2, 3, 5, 8 and 10 (and many others). These six countries alone account for roughly 2 billion people, almost three times as many as the fighter in second place on this basis (which, mainly because of China, happens to be the MiG-19).

So far these political and demographic comments have said nothing about the MiG-21 itself—though some might subscribe to the simplistic view that 'two billion people can't be wrong'. Again we in the West have a particular, and perhaps slightly distorted, viewpoint. The MiG-21 has invariably been 'the enemy', and when it has run up against the latest Western fighters it has usually come off second-best. Early MiG-21s seldom stayed to tangle with F-4s in Vietnam, and late-model MiG-21s were completely outfought by F-15s and F-16s over the Bekaa Valley. On this basis it would be easy to dismiss the MiG-21 as having been an also-ran throughout its long career.

Such a judgement would be unsound. So too would a judgement which claimed that the MiG-21 had always been as good as any other fighter, but that it has had the misfortune always to go into battle in the hands of unskilled and inexperienced pilots.

Where truth lies depends on who makes the assessment, and there is limitless scope for personal opinion and heated argument. It is obvious that the original MiG-21 of almost 30 years ago was an extremely marginal aircraft on the basis of weight, engine thrust and internal volume. Its original armament comprised two 30 mm guns, and when two small AAMs (copies of the Sidewinder) were added, one of the guns had to be removed. Gradually the MiG-21 grew in engine power, internal and external fuel and, especially, in armament; but it has throughout its life been a basically simple air-combat fighter, with extremely limited night and all-weather interception capability, and no pretensions about 'look down, shoot down' or 'blind first-pass attack' on surface targets.

It has many other shortcomings. At low altitudes it is (perhaps optimistically) regarded by its pilots as being able to 'hack it' with the best, and certainly to be able to outfly such opposition as an F-4 or Mirage III. But above 20,000 ft (6100 m) it becomes progressively less impressive, to the extent that even its pilots (and fighter jocks the world over rate their own aircraft better than they should) admit the fact. As for 'over Mach 2' performance, not many MiG-21 drivers have done it. There are now several accounts of 'flying the MiG-21' by pilots who do it for a living, and at least two accounts by top journalists given rides in two-seaters. Neither of the journalists went supersonic, and the professionals all discount Mach 2 (let alone the various figures in excess of that level). Limited internal fuel prevents the attainment of any Mach number beyond about 1.8 on any practical combat-type mission. Even greater is the discrepancy between the 'brochure' ceiling of 18 km (59,055 ft) and the greatest height that pilots can actually reach, which with the MF is around 46,000 ft (14,020 m).

How, then, should one assess the MiG-21? Leaving aside the fact that there are lots of different kinds of MiG-21, one can start with a firm foundation. The Soviet Union never buys defence hardware that is anything other than tough, soundly based and guaranteed to do its stuff in the harshest possible conditions. The basic aerodynamic design of the MiG-21 was in its day about the best that could be contrived. The thin delta wing gave the lowest supersonic wave drag and the lowest structure weight, and the addition of a powered 'slab' horizontal tail dramatically improved low-speed agility and field length in comparison with tailless deltas such as the Mirage III, which have to take off and land with their trailing-edge controls deflected upwards, forcing the aircraft downwards just when it most needs extra lift. The nose inlet with conical centrebody solves the problems of efficient pressure recovery at supersonic speeds and at all angles of attack, whilst simultaneously providing a neat place to put the small radar.

The MiG-21 was area-ruled from the original Ye-4 prototype onwards, though addition of bulky underwing stores, such as tanks, has always had a relatively large effect on this quite small and stumpy aircraft. The fact that the shape has been tinkered with so much, in the matters of fin chord, airbrake geometry and spine volume, is in no way indicative of a faulty design. Each change marked the attainment of a different objective.

Special mention must be made of the tremendous work of the Tumanskii engine bureau. Like SNECMA and Dassault's Mirages, this engine KB has (except for the odd prototype) been the monopoly supplier of engines for all the supersonic MiG fighters, as well as other important combat aircraft. In consequence it is the biggest engine KB in the Soviet Union, and its designs outnumber all other jet engines in today's world. Moreover, whereas SNECMA's Atar, basically a 1946 design, powers all the delta Mirages except the 2000, Tumanskii has developed a succession of ever better and more powerful engines to make possible a 30-year programme for the MiG-21.

If it had been restricted to the original R-11 engine, even in improved forms, it is doubtful that many MiG-21s would be flying today. When your engine partner keeps saying 'Have some more thrust . . . . less weight . . . . reduced specific fuel consumption . . . . fewer parts-count . . . . longer overhaul life' you are well on the way to keeping your basically old fighter in production for 30 years. Some Western analysts have got the cart before the horse in suggesting that in each major development stage the sequence was: airframe design change adding to gross weight, followed by panic realization more thrust was needed, followed by urgent design of a new engine. What actually happened was precisely the opposite, and in 1969 Mikoyan told the author that each new engine had been qualified for production in parallel with each new generation of MiG-21. The Russians are methodical, and wherever possible avoid last-minute panics.

On the other hand, it may be possible to overdevelop a basically good fighter. In a recent issue of *Air International* Roy Braybrook writes 'it may be suspected that (like the Bf 109) the MiG-21 became somewhat overloaded towards the end of its development'. The Bf 109 likewise worked its way through four types of engine, each more powerful than the last, in order to try to stay competitive. The author has no hesitation in criticizing the development of that famous World War 2 fighter, which got progressively more unpleasant to fly and never did cure its major deficiencies (apart from at last getting a geared rudder tab). The story of the MiG-21 is almost the direct opposite. The MiG designers were not so much trying to rectify faults as add extra capability, and so far as the author knows the last MiG-21 is as nice to fly as was the first.

Apart from switching to blown flaps the wing of the last MiG-21 is almost the same as the wing of the first, but almost everything else has altered. Few fighters can exhibit such a succession of changes as the MiG-21's dorsal spine, each successive version of which was a sensible answer to a current problem. The author has no doubt that, before 1975, the MiG OKB was looking at yet a further design change to give a canopy like that of the F-15 or F-16. This would have cured one of the basic and enduring deficiencies—pilot view—but only at the expense of a little more drag which was obviously judged to be an unacceptable penalty.

It is always rash to jump to conclusions where things Soviet are concerned, but it is probably safe to conclude that the MiG OKB is so busy with the current production types, and new designs for the 1990s, that not much effort is being put into further upgrades of the MiG-21. Meanwhile, in the European theatre at least, its numbers are inexorably dwindling (to an estimated 600 in Soviet Frontal Aviation in mid-1986). For many years the thing about the MiG-21 that most worried the West was its sheer quantity.

Elsewhere it will go on for a long while yet, though the new generations are gradually taking over. Back in August 1962 the Indian Air Force sent ripples of shock round the Western world, and Britain in particular, by signing up not only to import the MiG-21 but also to build it under licence. Unable to comprehend the truth, which was the plain fact that the Indians studied every fighter on offer, evaluated those that seemed the best, and finally arrived at a carefully considered decision, British analysts jumped to the conclusion that 'the only possible reason for the choice must be low cost'. The author is reminded how, at the time, the Indian Air Attache in London said to him 'Your country had nothing to offer but the Lightning, which we assessed as having almost exactly the same capability in performance and weapons for three times the price and three times the fuel consumption'. A further factor was the Soviet fighter's basic robust simplicity, which Hindustan Aeronautics judged to be within their capability to make at a low price.

At about the same time the People's Republic of China took the even more difficult decision to build the MiG-21 without a licence. The decision was more difficult because relations between Moscow and Beijing had deteriorated to the point where industrial co-operation was no longer possible. As the only production MiG-21 available to the Chinese was a very early F-series, this was the version subsequently put into production, as explained in a chapter of this book. And not least of the many paradoxes surrounding the MiG-21 is that it is a slightly improved Chinese version of this 30-year-old design which remains in production to this day, and not any of the much later models!

The author would like to express his great debt of gratitude to many friends who have assisted. Outstanding among these are Nigel Eastaway, Mike Badrocke, Robert J Ruffle, William Green of Pilot Press and, not least, Osprey's tireless Aerospace Editor Dennis Baldry.

*Bill Gunston*
Haslemere, England, July 1986

# Chapter 1
# Confusion in the West

Today the MiG-21 is probably the world's best-known aircraft. People who are variously white, pink, yellow, brown and black are all familiar with it, and very likely have it in their own air force; millions of them would be hard-pressed to name any other aircraft. It thus requires quite a mental effort to picture the West's top fighter analysts deciding that it was the swept-wing 'Faceplate', that it was designed by Sukhoi (or Yakovlev) and that in fact Mikoyan's latest fighter was the giant 'Fiddler' (actually the Tu-28P)!

The root problem is, of course, the deeply rooted secrecy that pervades almost everything in the Soviet Union. The names given above were invented by the Air Standards Co-ordinating Committee, an agency of NATO. The Soviet aviation fraternity consider these names rather insulting; after all, we might be offended if throughout the Soviet Union the Tornado F.3 was the Tovarich-C, and the B-1B the Bolshoi-B. The NATO-invented names were, and remain, a necessary and unambiguous way of identifying and reporting Soviet aircraft whose true designations are unknown. Many readers will find this book hard going. To them there is almost no such thing as a MiG-21; to them it is a Fishbed. The author has tried to keep at least one foot in the real world, and has resorted to 'Fishbed' as rarely as possible. Indeed, on occasion the suffix letters added to identify different sub-types of 'Fishbed' appear to be erroneous or at least questionable.

Another problem is that we in the West are hooked on the idea of 'makes' of aircraft. We find it hard to comprehend a nationwide system of OKBs (experimental aircraft bureaux) which create the designs and the prototypes, which—if they win over the competition—go into series production at one or more of the GAZ (state aviation factory) complexes. The MiG-21 was designed in the OKB led by Artem I Mikoyan (pronounced 'mick-o-yarn') and Mikhail I Gurevich (pronounced 'G'r-ye-vich'). But when the prototypes appeared, nobody in the West knew this.

This is the more surprising in view of the obvious family resemblance of early MiG-21s to the MiG-19 (NATO 'Farmer'), to the extent that—until NATO code names became available—they were dubbed 'Super Farmers' by the Western press. Looking back from 30 years later it all seems rather obvious, but on 24 June 1956 it did not seem that way at all.

Hundreds of Western observers were present at Moscow's Tushino airport on that day to see the Aviation Day flying display. A few were armed with cameras with long telephoto lenses, and the first of the many puzzles is how it is that when the new prototypes began to appear not a single good photograph was taken—at least nothing good has ever been published, and keenly competitive periodicals such as *Paris Match* and *Die Stern*, as well as McGraw-Hill World News (for *Aviation Week*), printed the best they had. Thus, the author and all the other Western aviation writers had to base their assessments on pictures that were few in number and of unbelievably poor quality.

All that was known for certain was that the announcer had identified one or more of the four new fighters as 'the MiG-21' and others as 'products of P O Sukhoi's bureau'. Believe it or not, there were simmering arguments among the Western pressmen at Tushino about just what had flown past! Even the total of four was disputed, and it was by no means certain that there were two with swept wings and two with deltas. Perhaps the MiGs had the swept wings and the Sukhois the deltas? The similarity of the slender acutely swept wings to those of the MiG-19 tended to confirm this view. The confusion was compounded when, after further prolonged debate, it was agreed that the four fighters were not all the same size.

Over the ensuing three years nobody in the West appears to have had any real idea of what was what. The pathetic performance of the photographers in 1956 was underscored when the 1957 Aviation Day display was cancelled, and the 1958 event comprised a fly-past of civil aircraft only. The situation was not helped by the Western analysts. Having come to their own conclusions they then proceeded to airbrush the poor existing photos and make models to support their findings, while several 'experts' arose whose titillating injections can now be seen as pure invention. Typical of 14 articles known to the author which were pure fiction was a major feature published by *RAF Flying Review* in 1960. This contained detailed drawings of the MiG-21 as a swept-wing fighter, gave the span as 39 ft, the length as 56.4 ft, the engine as 'one large Mikulin-designed AM-3 axial-flow turbojet which has a dry rating of the order of 18,000 lb st and an afterburning thrust of some 22,400 lb', and the armament as one 37 mm and two 23 mm cannon plus 'four M-100A infra-red homing missiles'. These missiles were described in surprising detail, and were said to have 'first appeared during the Korean War'. The article, said to have been written with the assistance of 'Major G J Geiger USAFR' even gave the thickness/chord ratio of the MiG-21's wing and said the nose inlet had 'a central diffuser bevel to give a two-stroke diffusion'. Maybe Maj Geiger was really an authority on motor-bikes?

At an early stage, in September 1956, the NATO names 'Fishbed' and 'Faceplate' leaked out, followed shortly afterwards by 'Fitter'. One imagines the name-givers knew what they were about, but Air Standards Co-ordinating Committee reporting names are officially classified (!) and the officials were unable—except off the record—to assist the technical press to get it right. In desperation some turned to the bible, *Jane's*. The 1956–57 volume contained a photograph of 'one of three Sukhoi delta-wing research aircraft' and noted under the heading THE SU-? DELTA FIGHTER that 'a trio of experimental heavy fighters with delta wings' had appeared. A single picture (of the Sukhoi S-1) appeared, with the caption 'The MIG-21 (?) swept-wing fighter', and the brief text said merely 'In these aircraft the general layout of the MIG-19 has been retained but a new centre-section with a straight trailing edge is used ... Eyewitnesses have remarked that the new fighter appeared to be about 25% larger than the MIG-19'. Clearly in those days *Jane's* did not even know how to write 'MiG'.

This did not exactly help, and in the following edition the august annual contained a three-view of what had become the accepted MiG-21—'Faceplate', without any straight bit of trailing edge—as well as 'The Sukhoi Delta-wing Monoplane which is code-named Fishbed B'. This was said in the text to resemble the 'A' variant but to have blunted wingtips, and to lack the 'leading edge extensions' on the tailplane.

For three years many publications described the rear ventral fins as a 'bulge' and illustrated it as such. According to the British *Air Pictorial*, 'The bulge under the rear fuselage may indicate the presence of a rocket motor, although this could be a fuel tank or armament bulge'. Once someone had suggested there was a retractable rocket launcher 'aft of the nosewheel housing' this titbit appeared frequently. In late 1958 *RAF Flying Review* gave the armament as 'three semi-externally mounted 37 mm cannon which are believed to be of revolver pattern with an extremely high fire rate, and honeycomb launchers (*sic*) for 50 mm folding-fin unguided air-to-air rockets may be carried underwing.' At least nine publications gave the number of rockets in the 'retractable fuselage pack' as 18.

Confusion was a long time abating. In 1959 John W R Taylor arrived in the *Jane's* editorial chair, since when any nonsense in that great book has been conspicuously absent, but even he could do no more than report what the officials thought. Thus in 1960, in a hardback book (*Warplanes of the World*) he reported 'MiG-21 (NATO code-name: Faceplate) .... Faceplate was described as the MiG-21 by a Soviet commentator .... Fitter ... is said to be smaller than Faceplate.'

At last, on 9 July 1961, the Soviet Union once again put on a great Aviation Day flying display at Tushino. By this time the MiG-21 was a mature fighter in large-scale service; but the West continued in utter confusion. One of the more comprehensive accounts of the display was given by *Air Pictorial*, which frankly said 'At this point we must turn to the delta-winged fighters and admit our ignorance. Before 9 July we had heard much of the Mig-21 [*sic*] 'Faceplate', the very similar 'Fitter', and the Sukhoi Su-15 'Fishpot' and Su-16 'Fishbed' ...

One of the smaller classic reference books, *The Observer's Book of Aircraft*, really suffered trying to sort out the Fishplates and Flatbeds. Year by year its silhouettes reached a higher standard, until by 1962 the MiG-21 was outstanding (except for having lateral air brakes under the tailplane). It was, however, still the 'Faceplate'. Turning the page we found the delta-wing Fishbed. This was at last described as being 'in large-scale service'; but it was identified as the MiG-23. Perhaps we will let *RAF Flying Review* have the last word in this chapter—which, in case anyone is still in any doubt, concentrates on nothing but the reports that were 100 per cent nonsense. As late as 1963 it published one of the last drawings of 'MiG-21 Faceplate', with the comment that 'its success would appear to have been limited, as it seems to have been withdrawn from SovAF service and is being exported to India, Iraq and Egypt'.

# Chapter 2
# A red star is born

During the Korean war (1950–53) the hundreds of encounters between the MiG-15bis and the NAA F-86E and F-86F resulted in very one-sided scores. Indeed, the USAF originally claimed combat victories of 14:1 in their favour. Subsequent analysis has shown such figures to have been impossible, but the best research still throws up figures not less than 3.5:1 in the Americans' favour. This is despite the fact that the MiG-15bis was the equal of the F-86 in almost all aspects of performance, and its superior in such important factors as climb angle and rate, ceiling and, usually, turn radius. It also had much heavier guns with longer range and far more lethal ammunition (but fewer shots per second).

Soviet analysts were justified in ascribing the one-sided combat score almost entirely to differences between the pilots. Both the NII VVS (scientific research institute of the air force) and the TsAGI (central aerodynamics and hydrodynanics research institute) came up with very similar comparative figures for the F-86F and MiG-15bis, and by January 1953 these were confirmed by receipt of detailed information on the US fighter's combat performance. But all this was regarded as history. Back in late (possibly October) 1952 the VVS had drafted an outline requirement for several next-generation aircraft including a new air combat fighter. Its main tasks were to take on the Century series of USAF fighters, especially the F-100, and shoot down the B-52 and flight-refuelled B-47 bombers. A level speed of Mach 2 was suggested, chiefly because of the expected existence of the B-58 supersonic bomber.

This requirement was not issued immediately, but was refined for several months. By early 1953 it called for a fighter with the highest possible air combat performance. No specific numerical values were demanded apart from the Mach 2 speed, but manoeuvrability, climb rate and ceiling were specifically emphasized. The aircraft had to be simple and cheap to maintain, easily operated from front-line

airstrips, and able to fire accurately with cannon using a radar ranging sight. It was accepted that range would probably be short, and that the normal operational method would be close ground control in reasonably clear weather in daylight.

Since 1945 TsAGI had continuously researched advanced aerodynamic configurations. More than in any other country, the central state control of the Soviet Union enabled good configurations to be repeated by different aircraft OKBs (experimental construction, ie, design and prototype-build, bureaux) so that the best possible aircraft should be created as quickly as possible. It became common practice for two or more rival OKBs to build aircraft of similar shape but to different scales, either using engines of different sizes or different numbers of similar engines. This procedure has continued to this day, but its first important application concerned the '1953 fighters'.

At an early stage, before the spring of 1953, it was agreed that the MiG OKB would be assigned the new air combat fighter. P O Sukhoi's OKB would have offered competition, but on Stalin's order it was shut down in 1949. There was also a need for a larger fighter, to be developed in day versions to shoot down the F-100 and other 'big fighters' and as a night and bad-weather interceptor equipped with search radar, which the smaller fighter could not carry. Yakovlev's OKB was heavily committed and, Stalin being dead, Sukhoi was told 'come back, all is forgiven, you can take on the big fighters'. It was the existence of big and small aircraft, each in the same two contrasting shapes, that threw the West's intelligence into such disarray.

TsAGI probably studied dozens of possible configurations. Their task is to recommend 'best shapes', and a weakness of the Soviet system is that TsAGI is unconcerned about such things as airframe weight, manufacturing difficulty or any of the other factors concerned with real chunks of aluminium.

TOP
*A I Mikoyan (right) sitting with A S Yakovlev at the 2nd
Session of the 6th Supreme Soviet in December 1962. Both
were at that time twice Heroes of the S U*
*(Novosti)*

ABOVE
*Typical of the West's photographic quality at Tushino on
24 June 1956 is this near-silhouette of the Ye-5.
Newspaper half-tone doesn't help!*
*(Robert J Ruffle archives)*

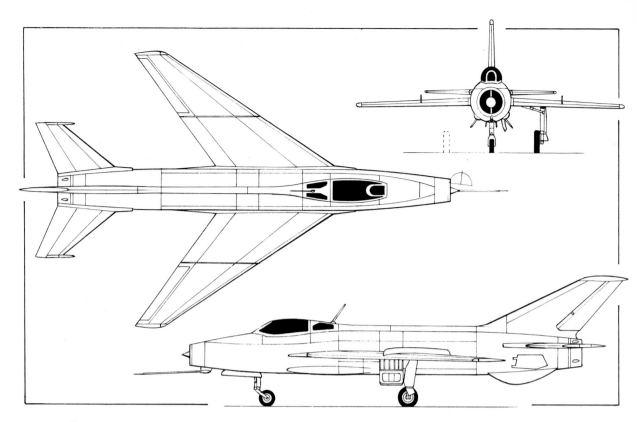

TOP
*A three-view of the Ye-2A swept-wing prototype, powered by a Tumanskii R-11 turbojet. No guns were fitted*

ABOVE
*The mixed-power Ye-50 was one of several MiG research aircraft in which a rocket was used to overcome lack of thrust from the main powerplant*
*(Tass)*

The author regrets that, on the one occasion he met Mikoyan, he failed to ask whether people in his position ever argued with TsAGI or resented being told what shape(s) to build their aircraft, or whether the imposition of a shape dictated by pure 'ivory tower' aerodynamicists threw up problems that compromised the final product. In any case Mikoyan was not among the Soviet designers who gave helpful answers to Western questions. Suffice to say that the philosophy endures, and the products do not seem to have suffered.

In fact in late 1953 TsAGI came up not with one

'best configuration', but two. One was the slender swept wing already used by the MiG OKB for the I-350, I-360 and MiG-19, with leading-edge sweep of 57° or 58° and outboard ailerons. This combination poses severe aeroelastic problems, and was avoided by NAA in the F-100 by the rather defeatist answer of putting the ailerons inboard and doing without flaps. The other was the delta, a pure triangle with leading-edge sweep again at 57°. In each case TsAGI put the wing almost in the ideal mid-position for minimum drag, and added a swept horizontal tail. This tail, from the start of design a one-piece slab because of

*Though clearly a sort of MiG-21, the original delta, the*
*Ye-5, was actually a completely different shape. The*
*tailplane root inlet shows prominently*
*(Robert J Ruffle archives)*

the success of the *stabilizator* developed a few weeks previously for the MiG-19S, was obviously essential for the swept wing. Its inclusion on the delta was the result of prolonged tests which showed the considerable benefits that resulted.

Previous deltas had often been tailless, the primary controls in pitch being elevons mounted on the wing itself. Experience by the British firms Gloster and Boulton Paul had confirmed the value of a separate horizontal tail, and TsAGI took the process further and discovered that if such a tail were included at the start then either field length could be reduced or the wing could be made smaller. The latter was unhesitatingly chosen, and TsAGI found that for equal field length their tailed delta had a wing area only 72 per cent as great as the tailless variety. Though comparisons between aircraft of quite different types are often misleading, one can get a first-order approximation of the difference by looking at the MiG-21 and Mirage III, the two wing areas (gross in each case) being 23 m$^2$ and 35 m$^2$.

TsAGI had played a major role in developing the swept wings of the MiG-15, MiG-17 and MiG-19, and refining the 58° swept wing for the new fighter was considered a straightforward task, though the new fighter was to be appreciably smaller than the MiG-19 and matched to the propulsion choice of a single R-11. In early 1954 this two-spool turbojet was well advanced in design at A A Mikulin's engine KB, though the actual design team was headed by S K Tumanskii, who had previously managed the design of the AM-5 engine for the MiG-19. Called TRD type R-37 by the VVS, the new engine was 50 per cent more powerful than the single-shaft AM-5, though it was almost exactly the same size; length was fractionally shorter, but diameter was increased from 813 mm to 828. A feature of all R-11 versions (except for a recent Chinese derivative) is that it is started on gasoline (petrol) drawn from a small starting tank on the compressor case. This eases the problem of good vaporization at low fuel pressures.

By the mid-1950s the MiG OKB had come to rely upon Tumanskii personally as a source of progressively improved engines. It was no blow to Mikoyan when, in 1956, Mikulin was removed in disgrace. Back in 1952 Mikulin had successfully given evidence against his old enemy, the aviation minister Khrunichyev, who was arrested and might have been executed. In February 1953 Stalin died;

Khrunichyev escaped sentence and later was set free, and he quickly settled the score with Mikulin and other adversaries. From the start of 1956 the engine KB was headed by Tumanskii, and the engines were redesignated. The AM-5 became the RD-9, and the new two-spool engine the R-11. Though Mikoyan did later build prototypes with Lyul'ka engines, he relied upon Tumanskii and his successors exclusively for engines for mainstream production aircraft, and in fact the Tumanskii succession of fighter engines over the past 30 years has no parallel in any other country.

While discussing personalities the point should be made that Mikoyan's partner, M I Gureyvich (the G in MiG) had been a sick man from 1950 onwards. Born 12 years before Mikoyan in 1893, Guryevich nevertheless remained Chief Deputy Constructor and did not finally retire until 1964. Mikoyan would have been the first to emphasize the role his more academic partner played in the MiG-21 programme. Ironically, the crushing workload borne by Mikoyan

resulted in his sudden death 'in harness' on 9 December 1970, while Guryevich survived him by six years!

Rather surprisingly the Soviet Union had never built a true delta. The TsAGI research showed that the triangular wing would have lower supersonic wave drag than any alternative form, would be structurally lighter and possibly give a higher ceiling, though the tunnel data here were conflicting. Called the balalaika wing from its shape, it was planned on the basis of the almost universal S-12 aerofoil profile, with a root thickness of 4.2 per cent and leading-edge sweep of 57°. Thanks to the tailplane it was possible to use flaps, and though these are often incorrectly called Fowlers there was no fixed wing above them and they are, in fact, track-mounted slotted flaps which give a slight increase in area as they come out and down.

There have been surprisingly few aircraft built in two versions made as identical as possible except for one major feature. In 1932 the Blackburn Biplane and

LEFT
*Using exactly the same aerodynamic input from TsAGI the bureau of P O Sukhoi designed the T-40, which led to this Su-9 interceptor, larger than the MiG-21*

BELOW
*With a job like his, why should Hero of the Soviet Union Georgii Mossolov worry about endangering his health? This portrait dates from 1963*
*(Tass)*

*The author has been told that '08' really was the eighth MiG-21 built, but the large buzz numbers painted on Soviet fighters usually merely identify each aircraft within a regiment or other unit*
*(Robert J Ruffle archives)*

Blackburn Monoplane were supposed to settle the arguments about which type of aircraft was better, but the technology was so primitive the monoplane showed no advantage. In the era following 1945 it would have been more instructive to build comparative aircraft with different wings or other variations, yet the mid-1950s series of Soviet prototypes—one lot by MiG, the other by Su—remain almost unique in history. It was an open secret in the MiG OKB that the delta was expected to show a clean pair of heels to the swept wing, and there was considerable eagerness to get aircraft in the air. Oddly, subsequent Western writers spent much time pontificating on whether the 'opposing factions' were within the design bureau, or between the MiG team and TsAGI, or what. Mikoyan simply told the author that there was never any question of 'opposing factions'. Paraphrased, he said 'We didn't know which wing would be best, so we built both'.

Mikoyan's bureau designated the swept-wing aircraft the Ye-2 (written 'E-2' in Cyrillic characters) and the delta the Ye-4. The assigned pilots were V P Vasin, G K Mossolov and V A Nyefyedov for the Ye-2 and OKB chief pilot GA Sedov for the Ye-4 and other deltas. Mikulin advised Mikoyan that, despite the R-11 being his top-priority engine, it would not be ready for flight in fighters until 1956. Sedov in fact was detached to Mikulin (later Tumanskii) to assist with the engine's development from the pilot's viewpoint, but Mikoyan determined to get prototypes flying at the earliest possible date. Accordingly the Ye-2 and Ye-4 were modified on the drawing board to be powered by the AM-5Ye (later designated RD-9Ye), with a takeoff thrust with afterburner of only 8,377 lb (3800 kg), only a little more than the earlier AM-5 version then powering the twin-engined MiG-19. This required a reduction in cross-section of the whole engine inlet duct. Mach 2 would be far out of reach with the less-powerful engine, and Mikoyan received permission to add another experimental prototype similar to the Ye-2 but with a rocket engine to boost the speed very considerably. Curiously, this received the designation Ye-50.

For many years the author had believed that this mixed-power aircraft was, in fact, the first to fly. Amazingly, a recent frank and informative account by V Kondratyev, who knows the facts but might possibly be the victim of slipshod typesetting and proof-reading, states that the first flight was made by the Ye-2, flown by Mossolov, on 14 February 1954. This is more than a year earlier than the author had previously believed possible, and suggests that the basic design, re-tailored to the smaller engine, must have been complete in spring 1953. Confirming the date, Kondratyev comments that it was not until two years later that Sedov took off in the first prototype with a delta wing.

At first glance this seems strange, to put it mildly. Not only was the *treugolnyi* (three-angled) wing regarded as likely to be the final winner but it was also the one that was least-known and likely to require the longest development programme. On reflection, the Soviet innate mood of caution and of careful plodding would indeed have put the traditional wing in the air first. What remains surprising is that the 57° delta was not tested in the meantime on some other aircraft, even if only at subsonic speeds. Such testing was never carried out, except of course with models in tunnels. Incidentally by 1954 not only did the MiG OKB have one of the first supersonic tunnels outside TsAGI, but Mikoyan also requested and was granted permission to create a really large and powerful experimental laboratory, with hundreds of workers in many departments, headed by A V Minayev. Subsequently this organization, certainly the biggest attached exclusively to any one OKB, has concentrated increasingly on systems, flight-control problems and electronics.

Everyone in the OKB knew that, should they succeed in satisfying the demand for a new fighter, it would become the MiG-21. The official service designations normally follow a rigid pattern, fighters receiving odd numbers. Thus, everyone in the OKB talked about the *dvadtsat pyervogo* (21) as if they had already got a production aircraft. Though subsequently the MiG-21 was to compete for international sales against the Mirage and F-5, these were later designs. The true contemporaries of the MiG-21 were the Swedish Saab-35 Draken and American Lockheed F-104, and it is worth commenting that, while all were designed to do the same job, the F-104 had a wing area of 18.28 m², the MiG-21 of 23 m² and the Saab of 49.2 m²!

Incidentally, without having too many digressions, one must remember that the entire *dvadtsat pyervogo* programme was just one of several engaging the attention of the MiG OKB in the mid-1950s. The previous-generation MiG-19 was continuing to be developed, and the twin-engined SM-10, SM-12, SM-12PM, SM-12PMU and SM-50 were all extremely active projects, the SM-12s looking at first glance very much like rather bigger Ye-2 versions. Moreover, though Pavel Sukhoi had been tipped to get the 'big fighters', Mikoyan determined to fight him for them and built the massive and immensely fast I-1 (I-370), I-3 (I-380), I-3P, I-7K, I-75, I-75F, Ye-150 and Ye-152, culminating in the Ye-166 which gained a world speed record. When the occasional picture of some of these reached the West it further confounded the confusion. These great aircraft have only a brief place in this book (Chapter 11), and it is worth noting that the twin-engined Ye-152A was of such interest to the Chinese that they built their own version, the Shenyang J-8 ('Finback'), which some Western observers initially thought was some kind of grotesque stretch of the MiG-21!

On top of all this, the MiG OKB was saddled, rather against Mikoyan's will, with creating the first generation of stand-off cruise missiles for the Soviet heavy bombers. The missiles known to the West as 'AS-1 Kennel', 'AS-2 Kipper', 'AS-3 Kangaroo' and 'AS 5 Kelt' were all designed within the MiG OKB in the mid-1950s. This OKB has remained a leader in this field, using MiG-21 technology in later missiles.

Dates for the first flight of the Ye-50 and delta Ye-4 have not been disclosed, but both flew in late 1955, the swept-wing Ye-50 a few weeks before the delta. The Ye-50, assigned to pilot V P Vasin, had almost the standard small-duct fuselage but was also fitted with a ZhRD S-155 rocket. The Ye-4 had just the single RD-9Ye afterburning turbojet.

It is desirable at this point briefly to describe these prototypes, to form a baseline to the prototypes and production aircraft which follow. A notable feature was that, to an even greater extent than the F-104, they marked a firm stand against the tendency towards increasing size in fighters. During World War 2 Yakovlev had succeeded in firmly implanting small size and light weight in the Soviet mind as desirable attributes of all air combat fighters, and this has stood the MiG-21 in good stead over 30 years. A typical loaded weight for the early Ye-2 and Ye-4 prototypes was 13,272 lb (6020 kg), which was more typical of earlier 'first-generation' subsonic jet fighters, and much lighter than any of the supersonic rivals.

All known MiG-21 variants have a nose inlet of circular form, with a centrebody to give two-shock compression. The duct immediately bifurcates to pass on each side of the cockpit, though the fuselage cross-section is a vertical ellipse. Behind the cockpit the ducts come together again and pass down the centre of the fuselage to give a good entry into the engine. Structure is all aluminium alloy except for the four frames to which the wings are attached, which are high-strength steel. Immediately aft of the wing is a forged frame to which the rear fuselage and tail section is attached by 12 bolts, removed for changing the engine. The two-spar swept tailplanes were attached to steel spigots well above the mid-point of the rear fuselage. Immediately below the tailplanes were the airbrakes, basically resembling those of the MiG-17. The wing was mounted 4.7 in (0.12 m) below the mid-point of the fuselage, and in fact an exact 90° setting at this level resulted in the underside of the wing being horizontal and the upper surface having slight anhedral. Production MiG-21s in fact have very slightly greater anhedral, though not as much as shown in many Western three-views.

Both the swept and delta wings were designed with S-12 profile, though of course the delta offered greater root depth and therefore much more internal fuel capacity. Structure of the swept wing resembled the MiG-19, but the new delta had a spar at 33.3 per cent chord and two spars at right angles to the

fuselage running from the root to a strong rib at the point where the front spar met the main (swept) spar. This rib also carried the outer tracks of the flaps and the inner ends of the powered ailerons. The main gears were hinged in the angle between the main and front spars and retracted forwards so that the long legs were parallel to the front spar but behind it. The wheels rotated 87° on the end of the leg to lie vertically in the narrow space in the fuselage between the engine duct and the skin, the bay being closed by a single door hinged well out from the centreline to clear future centreline stores. To clarify the geometry, the main wheel remained almost exactly upright and aligned with the aircraft longitudinal axis while it was carried on the end of the leg pivoting diagonally inwards and forwards. The levered-suspension nose gear retracted forward between the inlet ducts. Fuel was housed in a row of six cells in the fuselage and, in the delta aircraft, an integral tank in each wing (later, two tanks in each wing). Intended armament was two or three NR-30 guns, plus a drop tank or bomb on the centreline.

TsAGI was very concerned about maintaining good axial airflow across the wings, and most Soviet fighters at this time had large fences. The swept wing was given a very deep fence right across the upper surface from the leading edge to the flap, at 50 per cent semi-span. The delta was fitted with no fewer than three fences on each wing, and though these were not as enormous as that of the swept wing they

*Parked next to an Su-9 this cutaway AS-1 cruise missile was used for instruction before going to the Monino museum. Note the folded wing*
*(Maj Lennart Berns)*

extended round the leading edge to terminate on the underside. The innermost fence terminated at about 50 per cent chord, the others continuing right across the fixed part of the wing. Bearing in mind that fences are aerodynamic crutches that cause significant drag, it can be seen that everyone hoped that in due course this hideous array might be simplified.

TsAGI also warned Mikoyan about directional stability at high supersonic Mach numbers. The OKB had just begun to use rear ventral fins, and these appeared in primitive form on the Ye-2 and Ye-50. Little more than strakes, they were similar to the shallow keel used on MiG-19s. The author has never seen a photograph of the Ye-2 in its original form, but it seems fair to conclude that it suffered from yaw instability and snaking or Dutch roll at high Mach numbers. This problem may not have been encountered until after the Ye-50 had been built, because this aircraft was originally completed with the usual shallow ventral strake, on each side of which was a stainless-steel drain/jettison pipe for the concentrated nitric acid rocket oxidant. The S-155 rocket ran on acid injected together with kerosene from the main tanks, and was neatly installed at the base of the vertical tail, which was modified by having an extended dorsal fin and a smaller rudder.

Nothing has been revealed concerning flight testing of the Ye-2, which first flew on 14 February 1954, but it must have been slower than the MiG-19. In contrast the Ye-50, with the rocket in action, reached 2460 km/h (1,529 mph), or Mach 2.31. Apart from the British F.D.2 no other European aircraft was more than *half* as fast, and Vassin later wrote that the Ye-50 was 'very exciting'. It reached 20 km (65,600 ft) in 9.4 minutes from releasing the brakes, which was again beyond the capability of any other European aircraft over 30 years ago. Range, however, was only 280 miles (450 km), certainly a very limited figure though the author has no information on whether this assumes use of the rocket, and how much.

Subsequently the VVS gave careful consideration to the possibilities of mixed-power interceptors, as did the RAF and Royal Navy in Britain and Dassault in France. Once the more powerful R-11 became available it transformed the performance of the new MiG prototypes and made a rocket much less necessary, yet Mikoyan was authorized to fit S-155 rockets into R-11 powered Ye-50A prototypes. In all the OKB flew a total of 12 mixed-power prototypes in this programme, quite apart from the quite different rocket engines (RU-01S and U-19) used in the much more powerful SM-12PMU and SM-50 already mentioned. Later almost the same U-19 rocket, but cloaked under the cover-designation of 'U-2', will appear in this book slung under the record-breaking Ye-66A.

Again we know nothing about the early testing of the Ye-4, the first delta, beyond the fact that nothing catastrophic happened. No photograph has emerged, but it is reasonable to assume that it was fitted with the six-fence wing as described. So the story must jump to the receipt of the first R-11 engines at the OKB in early spring of 1956. Swept and delta prototypes were completed and waiting, the former being the Ye-2A and the latter the Ye-5. Compared with the Ye-2 and Ye-4 they naturally had slightly larger noses and inlet ducts, but the difference in size of engine propelling nozzle was far more obvious, as we can see by comparing the Ye-50 with the R-11-engined machines. But a much greater change in appearance resulted from replacement of the shallow centreline ventral fin by two canted surfaces which can fairly be called enormous. Whether this was a decision by TsAGI or the OKB we do not know, but they clearly were determined to stamp out high-Mach snaking by brute force. For some reason at least seven sets of drawings appeared over the years, initially in the West, showing the Ye-2A and Ye-5 with totally different tails, the differences extending to the fin/rudder, tailplanes and ventral fins! As far as the author can determine the complete tail units were identical, though it is easy to imagine that the vertical tail of the Ye-2A was taller. The tailplanes remained high, and a new feature was that each was mounted outboard of a fairing downstream of a cooling-air ram inlet blowing into the afterburner bay. No armament was fitted to the Ye-2A, but the Ye-5 probably had two NR-30 cannons in separate blister fairings along the fuselage.

We have only one photograph of the Ye-5, and the odd thing is that the aircraft looks vaguely cruder and less attractive than the Ye-2A, though apart from the wings the two were probably almost identical. The root cause is probably—and this has not been said before—the author is convinced the delta wing in the Ye-5 and Ye-4 was mounted in the standard lower-mid position. The Ye-5 was first flown by Sedov on 16 June 1956 (a date given by *Zolnierz Polski* for the Ye-4), a bare eight days before its brief public appearance and almost exactly a month after Nyefyedov's first takeoff in the Ye-2A. Intensive testing on a growing number of prototypes continued throughout 1956. At least 20 aircraft in the '21' programme had flown by spring 1957, the majority probably Ye-5s. The delta wing is believed to have been picked in December 1956, a major factor being greater internal fuel capacity.

At first the Ye-2A was faster, speed of 1,181 mph (1900 km/h) or Mach 1.79 being reached by late summer of 1956. Curiously the Ye-5 proved slightly slower, but for some reason this was traced to 'air spillage from the inlet', though the inlet systems were supposedly identical. Ratings of the R-11 were 8,600 lb (3900 kg) dry and 11,240 lb (5100 kg) with maximum afterburner. At some point in development small suck-in auxiliary inlet doors were added on each side of the nose and immediately beneath the wing leading-edge root. (The fact they cannot be seen in the rather blurred pictures of the Ye-2A and Ye-5

*Looking like something from an old movie set, this dramatic—indeed extraordinary—photo of a Ye-6 crash could depict the death of Nyefyedov (Robert J Ruffle archives)*

does not mean they were not fitted even to these aircraft.) Both R-11 prototypes demonstrated climb to 10 km (32,800 ft) in 1.3 minutes, an excellent performance made possible partly by the light loaded weight of 13,780 lb (6250 kg), the Ye-5 being predictably slightly lighter than the Ye-2A. By late 1956 the Ye-2A had been worked up to 1940 km/h, but the Ye-5s had overtaken it and reached the 'magic' 2000 km/h. The OKB believed they were the first in the world to achieve this speed with a fighter prototype without a booster rocket, though the J79-powered F-104As, then flying, were rather faster.

The delta Ye-5s must have been severely handicapped by their array of fences, but these were retained on the next major standard of build, the Ye-6. This was in many respects a new design, though with major portions almost identical to those of the Ye-5. The Ye-6 was designed in 1957, following the decision of the VVS to adopt the MiG delta as the MiG-21. The OKB was authorized to proceed with prototypes of three future service versions: the Ye-6 led to the MiG-21, the Ye-6T led to the MiG-21F and the Ye-6U led to the MiG-21UTI (later redesignated MiG-21U) dual trainer.

The first Ye-6 flew in early 1958. In the author's opinion the most basic modification introduced with the Ye-6 was to move the wings and tailplanes down so that the wing was in the low-mid and the tailplanes in the mid position. This resulted in shorter main landing gears and a larger tank above the retracted wheels. At first the wings retained their six fences, but the previously pointed tips were clipped slightly. The fin was given a dorsal extension leading into the dorsal spine which had been a feature of all the prototypes. The afterburner bay cooling inlets were repositioned further forward and higher, but the tailplanes continued to stand slightly away from the fuselage on a raised platform with a kink at the oblique hinge axis. Bringing the tailplanes down resulted in relocation of the airbrakes. It was essential for the airbrakes not to affect trim, and, after one of the biggest efforts in the entire flight programme, these were split into three, two under the forward fuselage (with beautiful 'tin bashing' as they incorporated parts of the gun fairings) and one under the fuselage under the rear part of the wing. Yet another change was to replace the canted ventral fins by a single large fin on the centreline incorporating the brake-chute cable.

Like previous development aircraft the Ye-6s were built by the experimental construction section under chief engineer I I Rotchik (who has appeared as 'Ritschik' in an East German publication), using production-type tooling wherever possible. One of the more intriguing features of the early production MiG-21s appeared in the Ye-6 prototypes. From the outset Mikoyan had boldly sanctioned the use of a one-piece frameless canopy of blown acrylic, with an inserted flat bulletproof windscreen inside the forward section. The original design was almost identical to that of the Folland Midge, which was flown in August 1954 a year after its canopy design was published. The author believes that, as on the British aircraft, the original canopy hinged up at the rear. By the end of Ye-6 development a radical new idea had been introduced. The canopy was hinged at the front, and when closed pressed down on a large lever above the ejection seat, arming the seat for use. The rear of the canopy incorporated trunnions which came down on forged cantilever rods projecting on

each side of the seat so that, when the seat was fired, it took the rear of the canopy with it. About 0.25 sec after firing, the seat would have risen about its own length, the canopy by this time having rotated free from its front pivots and, travelling with the seat, serving as a windbreak for the pilot.

Unfortunately the seat was unable to save Nyefyedov, who was killed on the eighth flight of the first Ye-6 in early 1958. He was pulling G at high Mach when, because of severe mismatching between the inlet system and engine, the R-11 suffered explosive compressor stall and flameout. Nyefyedov tried to relight, but the gasoline starting tank was overheated and, the report claims, contained only vapour. On the dead-stick approach control was progressively lost, and the prototype crashed before the electrically driven standby hydraulic pump could take effect.

In the ensuing panic Mossolov managed further flight-control development while Kokkinaki greatly improved inlet behaviour with a three-position inlet centrebody, pushed fully forward at over Mach 1.8, and improved the two auxiliary doors under the wing leading edges. Mikoyan accepted the idea of fully duplicated hydraulic systems throughout, with total redundancy in the flight-controls. The engineer who proposed this was Rostislav A Belyakov, today's OKB head and creator of the great MiG-29 and 31.

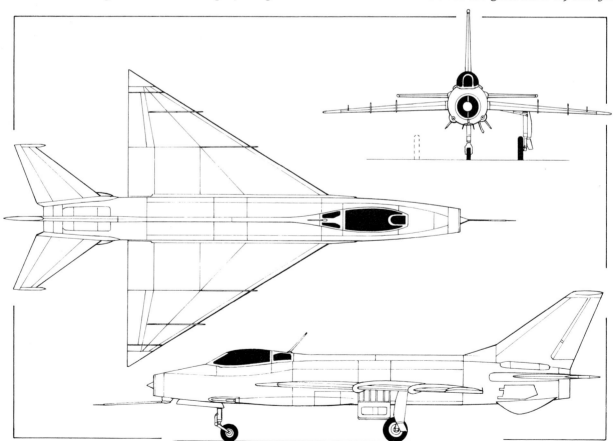

*The Ye-6/1 with initial airbrake/ventral fin configuration and three wing fences; note two NR-30 cannon*

# Chapter 3
# The MiG-21 and 21F

The transition from the Ye-6 of early 1958 to the service-cleared MiG-21 in 1959 is a part of the story not yet told. A few definite conclusions can be drawn from an external examination of the aircraft involved, but where Soviet hardware is concerned making deductions is historically fraught with difficulty. Even conclusions that seem obvious are often later shown to have been erroneous.

We do not even know how many Ye-6 development aircraft were built. We must not forget that at this time it was firmly believed in the West that the MiG-21 was the swept-wing 'Faceplate', and that the delta had fallen by the wayside. As late as 1962 Western writers were still reporting that the swept-wing aircraft had gone into service, though by this time the production was being described as 'a service evaluation quantity'. In fact the author has no evidence that any such batch existed, and Mikoyan assured him that no aircraft derived from the Ye-2 ever entered service with anyone.

Another misconception adhered to by Western analysts right through the 1960s was that the MiG-21 was just a stop-gap. It was so obviously limited in radius, endurance and firepower, and unable to operate in bad weather, that the general conclusion was that the 'real' MiG was 'Flipper', universally described as the MiG-23. One of the few Western periodicals to assess this aircraft correctly as 'only a prototype' was the author's own *Flight International* (issue of 7 November 1963). We further described its giant underwing AAMs as 'mock-ups'. Hardly had this issue hit the news-stands when we received a frame of 16 mm film showing the aircraft actually firing a missile, together with the cryptic comment 'Hardly a mock-up'. The author's boss was Editor 'Rex' King (Sqn Ldr H F King MBE) who in World War 2 had been one of the leading British air intelligence officers. After the most careful study and discussion we published the picture (28 November

1963) and described it as 'undoubtedly authentic'. It was, of course, a skilful fake. This family of large MiG interceptors of 1957–62 is briefly covered in Chapter 11. It included the aircraft in question (actually the Ye-152A), and this anecdote is added to underline how difficult it was at the time to assign the MiG-21 its enormous true importance.

In the preceding chapter we left the MiG OKB ruefully surveying the prospects after the fatal crash of the first Ye-6. This aircraft had a narrow-chord vertical tail faired directly into the dorsal spine, three small airbrakes, a single ventral fin with braking parachute on the left side just above it, slightly clipped wings with three large fences on each side, and a new canopy hinged at the front and with a large metal frame at the rear which pressed down on the seat arming lever. Aft of this opaque section the previous large rear-view transparency was replaced by two smaller sections, though rear view and aerodynamics were not significantly altered.

In the course of intensive Ye-6 flight testing in 1958–59 it was found possible to dispense with the six large fences and use just a single small fence on each wing near the tip, ahead of the outer part of the aileron which stops 400 mm, 15.75 in, inboard of the tip. This is one of the major puzzles of the MiG-21 development story. Bearing in mind the painstaking aerodynamic backup provided by TsAGI, and the fact that the pointed-tip Ye-5s had been flying some three years, one might have expected the drag-producing fences to have been sorted out long before, especially as—so far as the author can determine— the wing itself was not altered. The left and right wings had always been separate structures, attached at the root by precision bolts to four steel fuselage frames, leaving the interior of the fuselage free for the tanks and engine air duct(s). The root rib carrying the severe bending loads into the frames was kept at full depth at the front spar and faired by a root extension

projecting ahead of the leading edge. This was a feature even on the non-delta Ye-2 and 2A and has remained ever since, though no such fairing was needed on the larger MiG interceptors of 1957–62.

Eliminating the fences was entirely welcome, but at high Mach numbers—according to East European authors, in dives—the Ye-6 suffered instability (described, probably erroneously, as 'lateral' in some reports) which caused snaking. This resulted in further increase in fin area, and this process continued for almost 20 years! It is difficult to assess the situation correctly, because no good photograph is known of the Ye-6 and it is not possible to say with certainty whether it had two ventral fins, as did its predecessors, or (as the author believes) one. Certainly the pre-production MiG-21 had a single ventral fin and a small added dorsal fin linking the dorsal spine to the tail.

Another of the uncertainties concerns armament. The author finds it hard to believe that any of the early prototypes carried three 30 mm cannon, though certainly the Ye-6 had two. The bare NR-30 weighs 146 lb (66 kg), and according to most chroniclers it was purely to save weight and improve agility and flight performance that the left-hand gun was deleted. In 1958 the R-11F-300 engine was introduced, giving a welcome increase in thrust, and the author believes this coincided with the addition of wing hardpoints. Some authorities, such as *Flieger Revue* of East Germany, insist that the F-300 engine was fitted to the original Ye-6, but this was not possible. Almost certainly the Ye-6T, the prototype of the first series MiG-21 in 1959, was the first to have this engine. It brought an increase in engine nozzle diameter which resulted in a better shape for the rear fuselage. Though the author is unconvinced that Western side elevations of the earlier prototypes are

*Used for airshow demonstrations, this broad-finned MiG-21F was fitted with two underwing smoke generators. It was first seen in 1961*
*(Robert J Ruffle archives)*

accurate, with their sharply downswept rear-fuselage upper line, the Ye-6T was the first to have an ideal smooth profile all the way to the nozzle.

Thus by about mid-1959 the MiG-21F, the first series (production) version, was cleared for use by the VVS, and entered production at two GAZ which have not yet been officially disclosed, though they are believed to have been at Gorkii and Kuibyshyev. There was no production 'MiG-21' without the F suffix, the latter meaning *forsirovanni* or boosted. This reflected the increase in thrust of the R-11F-300 over the R-11. All the Tumanskii MiG-21 engines are listed in Appendix 1.

Externally almost the only distinguishing feature of the production MiG-21F was the increase in chord of the fin. This was done without changing the basic structure of the fin, nor the rudder and tailplane power units in its base. All that was done was add a new leading edge of almost wedge profile ahead of the front spar. This increased the chord, measured parallel to the longitudinal axis, by about 15 in (380 mm); the actual increase, perpendicular to the leading edge was 8 in (200 mm). The new fin leading edge intersected the dorsal fin at its mid-point, but most of the dorsal fin remained visible because it was wider than the new leading edge above it. Other additions included the two wing hardpoints, normally occupied by K-13A (Sidewinder copy) AAMs, a centreline attachment for a drop tank of 107.7 gal (490 litres) capacity, and a modified air-data boom whose rear attachment could be unpinned allowing it to pivot up around the front attachment through 18° to reduce the distressingly high number of ground damage accidents.

Before describing the MiG-21F it is appropriate to glance at various closely related research aircraft and prototypes constructed by the MiG OKB in 1958–60. Most important to the MiG-21 programme was the Ye-6U, first flown in February 1960. This was the first two-seater. Though basically a straightforward derivative of the Ye-6T, the 6U incorporated several new features. The main change was naturally the addition of a rear (instructor) cockpit, replacing the two forward fuselage tanks by one very small cell and requiring a much sharper inward curvature of the left and right engine air ducts. A one-piece canopy was designed to cover both cockpits, hinged to the right and remaining with the aircraft after ejection of the seats. Guns were omitted, and rather surprisingly the forward airbrakes were redesigned with smaller area. The main landing gears were of an enlarged type already produced for the next-generation Ye-7, though gross weight was actually slightly reduced, as explained in Chapter 9.

Among continuing mixed-power studies was one aircraft actually built, in 1958. The Ye-60 was the last of the non-deltas in this family, having a slightly modified 57° swept wing and a ventrally installed rocket engine; the latter has not been identified but was probably of the S-155 type. No photograph of the Ye-60 has been seen. The Ye-66 must have been an engine testbed with the airframe of the standard production MiG-21F-13 but a significantly more powerful engine. Mossolov used this aircraft to set the Soviet Union's first FAI-homologated world absolute speed record at 2388 km/h (1,483.83 mph) on 31 October 1959. Equivalent to about Mach 2.247 at high altitude, this caused a twinge of disquiet to Western analysts, and also interested the senior staff of the Indian Air Force which had been informed of a generalized Mach limit for the MiG-21 of 1.7. The

*Another view of the smoke-equipped MiG-21F, which had a single gun. It is seen with full left aileron applied. The smoke dispersion is extraordinary (via Pilot Press)*

TOP LEFT
*Bearing number 31, the Ye-66A set a world record for absolute altitude in 1961. Here it makes a low flypast with rocket engine operating*
*(Robert J Ruffle archives)*

ABOVE
*Another participant at the Tushino show on 9 July 1961 was this Ye-6 series development aircraft with assisted-takeoff rockets*
*(Robert J Ruffle archives)*

LEFT
*Numbered 01, this MiG-21F is not thought to be anything other than a normal series machine. Complete with drop tank it has long been in a Moscow museum*
*(via Robert J Ruffle)*

engine was reported to the FAI as the R-37F, and there seems no doubt it was the first flight-cleared example of the R-11-300, which introduced a larger afterburner giving increased supersonic thrust without change in dry rating. As explained in Appendix 1, this engine (oddly) appears to be more powerful than the R-11F-300 which preceded it, despite the letter F meaning 'boosted'. Another puzzle is that the aircraft displayed publicly as the Ye-66, and with number 66 painted on it (not that that means a thing), appeared to be a regular service 21PF, a later aircraft entirely, complete with wing pylons and AAM shoes!

Highest-flying of all MiG-21s, the Ye-66A was used by Mossolov to set an FAI-homologated world altitude record of 34,714 m (113,892 ft) on 28 April 1961. As photographs show, it was extensively modified, one would imagine as much for speed as for height. From the canopy to the tail it was rebuilt, with a long spine fairing the canopy into the wide-chord fin

(which was not identical to the fin of later series MiG-21s), and there were numerous detail changes elsewhere. The extra performance came from the installation of a 'U-2' rocket in a large self-contained nacelle under the fuselage, with the jet passing between large canted left and right ventral fins. The U-2 has never been publicly described, but there is no reason to doubt that it burned RFNA (red fuming nitric acid) and kerosene, the acid being housed in the front of the rocket nacelle and the kerosene being regular aircraft supply. Thrust, probably to some degree controllable, was given as 3000 kg (6,614 lb), probably a sea-level rating and equivalent to about 8,000 lb at high altitude. The Ye-66A displayed the number '31' and bore no relationship to the much later aircraft exhibited as the Ye-66. It is the author's belief that the PF with '66' painted on it was a typical Soviet joke, to see how many Westerners would jump to the erroneous conclusion that here at last was the Ye-66.

Practically nothing is known of the Ye-66B beyond the bald fact that it was a 1964 (not, as often reported, 1974) record version of the MiG-21F-13 fitted with two booster rockets, type 'TTPD'. The latter is an acronym for booster rockets, and not a type designation, and the author does not even know if they were both under the fuselage, under and above, or beneath the wings (very unlikely). John W R Taylor has surmised they might even have been assisted-takeoff rockets! Another record designation was Ye-33. This applied to an OKB two-seater, corresponding to one of the MiG-21U versions, which in May/June 1965 was used by women pilots to set class altitude records, as noted later.

The remainder of this chapter is a description of the MiG-21F-13, the first series version built in large numbers. It was manufactured under licence by the Aero Vodochody National Corporation in Czechoslovakia, without the local designation S-106 being used. Early Czech aircraft appear to have been identical to Soviet F-13s, the first example flying at Prague Vodochody on 9 May 1963. Output was maintained at about 40 per year for at least five years, and most of these aircraft had metal skin fairing the canopy into the spine. At least one aircraft built with a transparent fairing later appeared with shiny new metal skin here. An almost identical fighter was

TOP
*Another view of MiG-21F No 01, which for 22 years has been on outdoor display at Moscow's Central Museum of the Armed Forces. It is representative of the earliest production standard, with original fin (via Robert J Ruffle)*

LEFT
*One of the first batch of 10 MiG-21F-13s supplied to Finland in April 1963. Until this time the MiG-21 had been shrouded in mystery!*

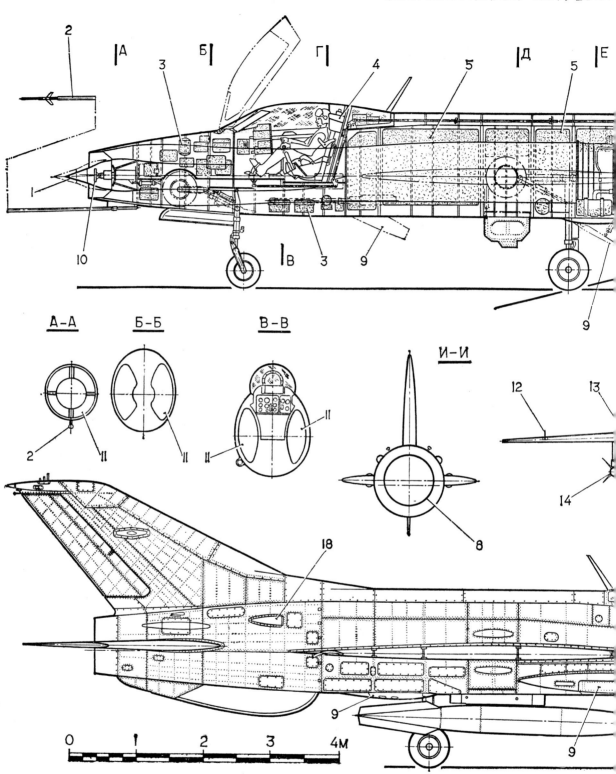

А-А   Б-Б   В-В   И-И

0   1   2   3   4М

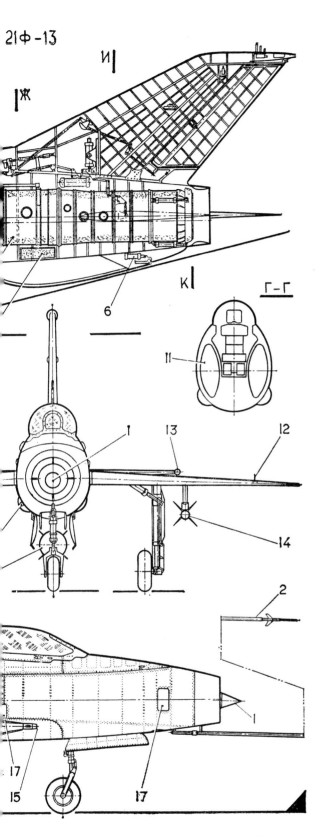

21Ф-13

*Though simplified, these drawings of the MiG-21F-13 were prepared with full official co-operation, and explode various myths perpetuated in Western cutaways. The engine is an R-11F-300 and the missiles K-13s (Modellist Konstruktor No 7)*

supplied to China in small numbers in 1960. After the severance of political ties with the Soviet Union the Chinese accomplished the remarkable feat of putting the MiG-21F into production, as outlined in Chapter 10.

### MiG-21F-13 description
### Wing

The MiG-21F, airframe Type 74, has a cropped delta wing described as mid-mounted, though it is actually slightly below the mid position. Left and right wings are made separately. Each is an almost pure triangle, with the leading edge swept at 57° and the trailing edge at right-angles to the fuselage. Ruling aerofoil is TsAGI S-12 series, with thickness/chord ratio of 4.2 per cent at the root and 5.0 per cent at the tip (which is cut off just short of the point). Mean aerodynamic chord is 4002 mm and chord on the aircraft centreline 5970 mm. Angle of incidence is 0°, and dihedral −2° (ie, 2° anhedral). Structurally the wing has a front spar at 33% chord, preceded by 26 ribs at 90° to the leading edge, joined to a rectangular rear section with main and rear spars at 90° to the fuselage and 12 ribs. The main gears fold into the triangular space between the front and main spars, as described later. Immediately behind the main leg bays are the landing lights, recessed into the lower skin on hinges.

Materials include D16 duralmin, light alloys V-95, ML5-T4 and VM-65, and 30KhGSA high-strength chrome steel. Upper and lower skins, each in five sections, are of V-95 in thickness from 1.5 to 2.5 mm. The inboard part of the main triangular wing box forms integral tanks. There are no integrally stiffened machined panels, but the entire structure of the wing box, including both skins, is chemically milled to achieve the ideal stress distribution for minimum weight and without machining scratches. Both wings are offered up to eight root attachments at five fuselage stations. Ribs 13 and 15 ahead of the front spar have bosses to which are attached the underwing pylon. Rib 19 serves to protect the wing during ground transport. Inside the leading edge are non-linear push/pull rods which control the aileron hydraulic power unit between the spars. Each aerodynamically balanced aileron has an area of 0.44 m², the left aileron having mass balance; aileron deflection is ± 20°. Between ailerons and root are the rectangular flaps, similar to the Fowler but with no fixed wing surface above. Each has an area of 0.935 m², and are lowered to 24.5° on takeoff and to 44.5° on landing. Ahead of the outer part of each aileron, 670 mm from the tip, is a fence with a height 7 per cent of local chord. Each wing contains 20 maintenance access hatches with screwed covers.

### Fuselage

The fuselage is a simple light-alloy semi-monocoque of oval cross section, made in front and rear portions joined at Frame 28. After undoing structural and service connectors the whole rear end can be removed at Frame 28 to expose the entire engine. The main fuselage has load-bearing frames at Stations 2, 6, 11, 13, 16, 16a, 20, 22, 25 and 28, and these are joined by main longerons and a small number of stringers in supporting the relatively thick skins. Ruling materials are D-16 and V-95, with joints and point loads carried by machined forgings in 30KhGSA and 30 KhGSNA steel. The rear fuselage has 13 frames, Nos 28a, 34, 35a and 36 being load-bearing. The skin is mainly D-16ATM in 1.2 mm thickness, though hottest parts are steel.

Most of the fuselage incorporates an internal engine air duct. This begins circular, bifurcates almost at once to go past the cockpit, and then quickly returns to a circular tube on the centreline to present a smooth airflow to the engine. The actual inlet has one of the first variable conical centrebodies, in which the radar is installed. The entire forward section including the conical radome is arranged to slide in and out axially in order to focus inlet shockwaves and match airflow to the engine's demands. Throughout all normal flying the cone is retracted; at Mach 1.5 it smoothly translates to the intermediate (first extended) position, and at Mach 1.9 it moves fully out to the second extended position. The inlet control system is governed by air density and absolute temperature using the air-data sensors on the nose of the aircraft, and also by engine rpm and power demand. In the second extension (fully out) position the inlet area is held to below 0.93 of the maximum. The same control system also operates the spill doors on each side of the nose through which excess airflow is dumped overboard when the inlet supply exceeds engine demand. Below the leading edge of the wing roots are simple suck-in auxiliary inlets which admit extra airflow whenever the engine is run at high power at low airspeeds, as at takeoff.

The engine installation and cockpit are described separately. The main air-data probe is mounted at the bottom of the nose, aft of which is the bay for the nose landing gear. Further aft are the two fun installations, only that on the right normally being used, and the rear part of each of these blister fairings is incorporated into an airbrake of 0.76 m$^2$ area, driven hydraulically to a maximum angle of 25°. Further aft, inboard of the wing roots, are the compartments for the retracted main wheels. Further back still under the fuselage is a rear airbrake of 0.47 m$^2$ area, driven hydraulically to 40°. Still further aft, beside the ventral fin, is the compartment for the braking parachute. In the fuselage are 111 service openings seated by hinged or screwed covers.

## Tail
Fabricated of conventional light-alloy parts, with flush-riveted skin, the tail comprises a fin, rudder, left/right one-piece tailplanes (horizontal stabilizers) and a fixed ventral fin. Each tailplane has a symmetric A6A profile of average 6% thickness/chord ratio, with an anti-flutter mass faired ahead of the tip. Leading-edge sweep angle is 55°, angles of dihedral and incidence 0°, span 3.552 m and area (each half)

4.45 m$^2$. Maximum tailplane deflections are $+7.5°$ and $-16.5°$. The vertical tail has a symmetric profile of S-11 type, with a t/c ratio of 6%, and (discounting the small dorsal fin) a leading-edge sweep of 60°. Fin skin is 0.4 mm thick, but the rudder, of 0.965 m$^2$ area, has 0.8-mm skin and is power driven to 25° left or right. The ventral fin, extending along almost the whole length of the removable rear fuselage, has a maximum depth of 352 mm.

## Landing gear
The tricycle landing gear has single struts and wheels, track and wheelbase being respectively 2.692 m and 4.810 m. The castoring nose unit has a tyre 500 × 180 mm, with a pressure of 0.58 MPa, and is fitted with an anti-skid twin-shoe brake using bottled air passed through a reducing valve set to 1.02 MPa. The wheel has levered suspension multiplying the stroke of the oleo. The main units have tyres 660 × 200 mm, with pressure adjustable from 0.78–1.01 MPa, and are fitted with anti-skid disc brakes using air reduced to 1.56 MPa pressure. Steering is by differential braking. Each vertical shock strut is pivoted to a trunnion mounted diagonally in the base of the outer end of the main spar. The retraction jack pulls the unit diagonally in and forwards, the wheel being simultaneously rotating through 87° relative to the leg to preserve its original orientation to lie fore-and-aft vertically in the side of the fuselage.

## Powerplant
The R-11F-300 two-spool afterburning turbojet is an outstandingly simple and robust engine which in many ways was the most advanced of its era. One of its advanced features was that it has no inlet guide vanes, the first LP compressor stage being overhung ahead of the front bearing. Another feature by no means common in the 1950s was completely smooth variation of thrust from ground idle to maximum afterburner, all under single-lever control. Yet another was an automatic starting cycle initiated by pressing a single button, with automatic limitation of temperatures and other variables.

The basic engine weighs 1,182.2 kg complete with starting and control systems. Overall pressure ratio is modest, because there are just six compressor stages, three LP and three HP, each spool driven by a single-stage turbine. There are several interlinked auxiliary systems. Engine lubricating oil is totally self-contained, and cooled by fuel. The fuel pump has its own extremely precise regulator which holds engine rpm constant through all variations of altitude and airspeed. The afterburner fuel pump, capable of very high flow rates, permits the afterburner to ignite at an extremely small additional fuel flow, giving light-up imperceptible to the pilot. An auxiliary oxygen injection system is carried to ensure reliable inflight ignition following flameout at high altitudes. The starting system is entirely electric, and relays ensure the correct sequencing of events without dangerous excursions of temperature. An electrically signalled hydraulic subsystem controls variation of area and profile of the propelling nozzle. Sixth-stage bleed air is fed to the cockpit environmental control system and the tanks for fuel, starting fuel and hydraulic fluid. The main accessory gearbox under the compressor case carries nine driven units which include a starter/generator, two hydraulic pumps, an air compressor and tachometer generator.

The installed engine has its compressor inlet face butted against a rubber seal at frame 22 and it extends aft to the extreme tail of the fuselage. The engine is surrounded by six sealed chambers each bounded by a frame with a rubber seal pressed against the engine. The main weight of the engine is taken by an overhead mount at frame 25, and the rear mount is at frame 28.

## Cockpit

The comfortable cockpit is pressurized and air-conditioned to an equable temperature. The SK ejection seat can be used at all heights above 110 m and up to an indicated airspeed of 1100 km/h. The one-piece blown-acrylic canopy is pivoted to the fuselage at the front and when closed rests at the rear on lugs projecting on each side of the seat. In a normal ejection the pilot fires the seat, which via the rear locating lugs lifts the canopy away with it, rotating it about the front attachments until it forms a windbreak protecting the pilot against the air blast. Rotation about the front attachments frees the canopy from the aircraft, so that it travels with the seat for some distance before separating. Rotation of the canopy could cause it to be forced against the head of a tall pilot, and this is prevented by a preset arm on the seat headrest. The pilot can elect to use a sequenced ejection in which the seat is fired a fraction of a second after jettisoning of the canopy.

In most F-series subtypes there is a fixed transparent portion of fuselage deck downstream of the canopy. Little need be said concerning the conventional instrumentation and controls. Above the main panel, which is vertical and very deep, is a three-ply slab of armoured glass 62 mm thick. Further protection is afforded by the thick planks on frames 6 and 11 and the armour on the seat headrest.

## Systems

Fuel is housed in a group of six tanks of T-6 aluminium in the fuselage, with capacities of 235, 660 + 60, 265, 200 and two of 240 litres. Further fuel is carried in the wing integral tanks, two of 175 litres and two of 110 litres. Of this total of 2470 litres, 2340 (515 Imp gal) is usable without any stability problems. A further 490 litres can be carried in a drop tank on the centreline pylon.

There are two totally independent hydraulic systems, each energized to a maximum pressure of 20.59 MPa by a variable-displacement pump on the engine accessory gearbox. The hydraulic systems are used to translate the nosecone in and out, operate the inlet spill doors, retract and extend the landing gear, drive the flaps, adjust the jetpipe nozzle, open the airbrakes and work the flight-control surfaces. In emergency an electrically driven standby pump is cut in automatically, providing sufficient power for safe return to base. Flight controls are generally conventional, with push/pull rods conveying the pilot demands to the surface power units. The tail control rods pass along the dorsal spine, and the tailplane power unit is located in the fin, driving the surfaces via backlash-free rods and levers. Automatic q-feel is provided to tailor surface deflection according to indicated airspeed.

The pneumatic system consists of a main circuit and an emergency circuit. The main system serves the wheel brakes, raising of the canopy, inflation of the peripheral canopy seal, jettisoning of the canopy in emergency, inflation of the pilot's partial-pressure anti-G suit, loading and cocking of the cannon, shutting-off of the main fuel stopcock, various deicing functions and release and ejection of the braking parachute. The emergency circuit provides for standby extension of the landing gear and operation of the wheel brakes.

The starter/generator serves as the primary source of electric power, but emergency and reserve power is drawn from two AG/Zn (silver/zinc) batteries which have sufficient stored power to ensure an engine start under the most adverse Siberian conditions with no external power. Inverters and AC subsystems provide 115-volt single-phase supply at 400 Hz and 36-volt three-phase, again at 400 Hz frequency, for the avionics, instrumentation and anticing functions.

The oxygen system for the pilot and for high-altitude relights is of the gaseous type. The bottles are grouped inside the wing roots. Windshield anti-icing is accomplished by an alcohol spray with additives to prevent the supply itself freezing.

## Avionics

The standard basic tactical installation of 1960 includes the UKV VHF radio (duplicated) and the RSIU UHF for fighter communications, the former using an inclined blade aerial behind the cockpit and the latter left/right aerials scabbed on the sides of the fin. SRO-2 or -2M IFF (identification friend or foe) uses the usual group of parallel rods of different lengths above the top of the fin and, optionally, under the forward fuselage. Late-production MiG-21Fs have an SO-69 RWR (radar warning receiver) covering the rear hemisphere via diagonal receiver aerials on the sides of the aft-pointing fin tip above the rudder. The SV radio compass is standard, and the horizontal dipole aerial for the RV-2 radio altimeter—used only at low levels below 300 m AGL—is installed below either wingtip (usually the left) and is occasionally found beneath both tips. The simple radar in the inlet centrebody transmits a fixed pencil beam, boresighted along the aircraft longitudinal axis, and provides target distance only. This is automatically fed to the gyro gunsight. It has only a limited capability as a target detection and location device, though even this early MiG-21 variant is

E-E

Л-Л

Д-Д

Ж-Ж

М-М
УВЕЛИЧЕНО

Н-Н

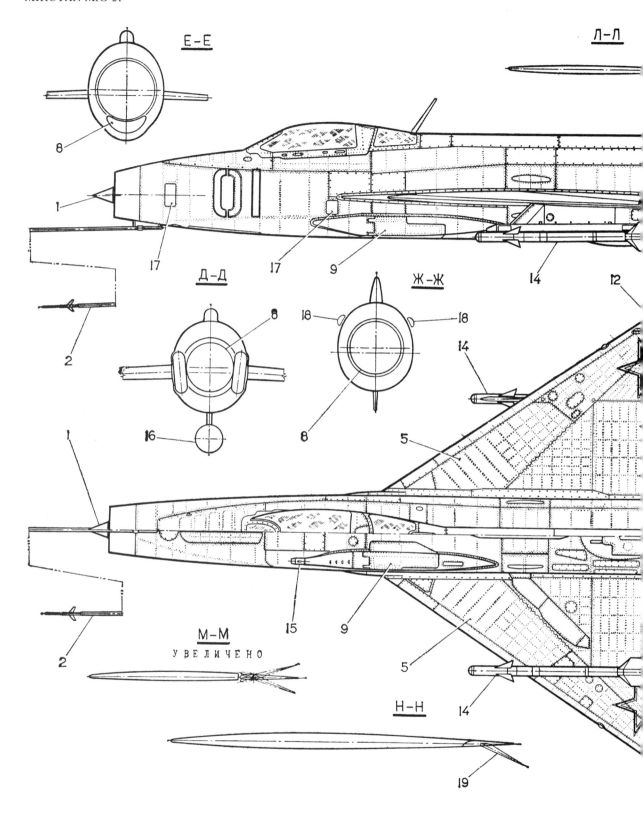

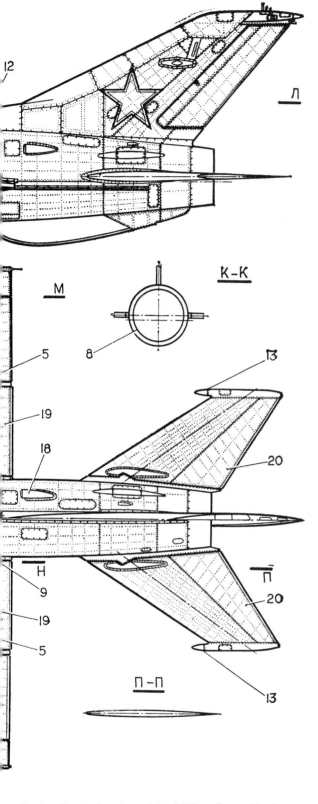

12

Л

M

K-K

5

8

19

18

13

20

H

9

20

19

П

5

П-П

13

*Further Soviet drawings of the MiG-21F-13, this time showing the exterior. The plan view shows the starboard half of the aircraft from above*

described as having the ability to operate by day or night 'even in bad weather conditions'.

**Armament**

The only inbuilt armament normally comprises a single NR-30 cannon of 30-mm calibre, mounted in the lower right side of the fuselage. The 75-round box of ammunition is loaded straight through the side of the fuselage between the gun and the wing root. Under each wing, on leading ribs 13 and 15, is the pylon for external stores. The most common are the UV-16-57 rocket launcher, housing 16 rockets of 57-mm calibre, and the K-13A air-to-air missile (derived from the American AIM-9B Sidewinder). Other common loads include the S-24 rocket of 240-mm calibre, various GP bombs up to FAB-250 (250-kg) size, bomblet dispensers, napalm and chemical weapons. No weapons are carried on the centreline pylon, which is used only by the drop tank.

# Chapter 4
# The F in service

Though small numbers of early MiG-21F fighters did reach IAPs (fighter regiments) in late 1959, it was 1960 before the type was declared operational. So far as the author knows, all MiG-21 deliveries in the Soviet Union have been to the gigantic FA (Frontal Aviation, or tactical air force). It is possible that a handful may have gone to the AV-MF (naval air force) as advanced combat trainers, but apparently none was supplied new to the IA-PVO (manned interceptors of the air defence forces). No Soviet MiG-21 pilot has defected, and by mid-1985 none had written in any useful detail about his equipment, so from the operational viewpoint we must turn to other sources.

Total deliveries of all versions to the FA exceed 6,000, at least half this total being attrition buys initially put into storage. Thus, about 3,000 went straight from the GAZ to an IAP, but of this total probably only about 900 were MiG-21Fs. By the time the fighter's development was completed—and though quite normal by Soviet standards, it was very protracted in comparison with that of most Western fighters—it was clear that this initial version could be improved, as explained in the next chapter. Deliveries were therefore relatively modest, though one suspects that every effort was made to export this version and certainly the number of MiG-21Fs exported ran far into four figures, or well over the number kept at home. Interestingly, since 1981 large numbers of aircraft able to be used for interception have been transferred from the FA to the PVO, and this includes several hundred MiG-21s, some of them with very little flying time. All are of types much later than the MiG-21F, which remains in Soviet service only as an advanced fighter-pilot trainer and as a popular hack for deskbound officers and for trials programmes. The Soviet Union has usually been reluctant to scrap any weapons withdrawn from a successful service career, and it

may well be that most of the Soviet MiG-21Fs still exist. By Western standards they are probably little-used, because until recently Soviet pilots generally did less flying than their Western counterparts. A contributory factor was the overhaul life of engines and systems hardware, typically one-tenth that of Western equivalents because of deliberate Soviet policy.

The author was told that no MiG-21 simulator was thought necessary until well after 1965, and that pilot conversion was always carried out almost entirely with classroom lectures and, following checks in the MiG-15UTI and MiG-17, actual flight in the various types of MiG-21U trainer. Moreover, throughout most of the combat career of the MiG-21 in Soviet service the instructional methods adhered to the old Soviet style. The syllabus assumed that the pupil had not only an almost total lack of experience or understanding of fighter aircraft but also an inability to learn except by rigorous repetitive instruction over a long period. Thus the course moved at what a Western pupil would think a snail's pace, laying down the law not only in the most meticulous detail, so that the pupil was almost told how to control his exact hand or head movements, but also insisting on extremely conservative operating procedures. We are told by many non-Soviet pilots who attended the schools for 'foreign combat pilots' at Tashkent and Lugovaya that, among other restrictions, there was a total prohibition on instrument flying or entry to cloud, exhibition of any kind of initiative, or the slightest departure from the strict procedures. The latter insist on an extremely long flat approach from an enormous circuit, and, in the case of most MiG-21s, prohibition on use of full flap on landing.

This is a good place at which to offer an assessment of the MiG-21F in the context of its times. First, we have to divorce ourselves from the plethora of wildly inaccurate Western assessments, which at first

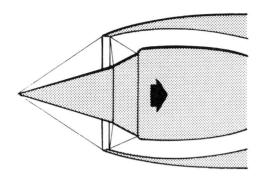 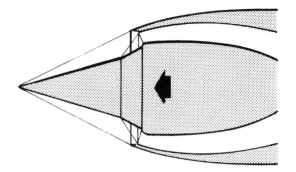

*Based on a Soviet drawing, these simplified cutaway views show how the pattern of shockwaves (very thin lines) varies as the two-angle conical centrebody is translated in and out of the inlet; the conical centrebody is the only part which moves*

ABOVE
*Late production F-13s of the LSK (East German air force). The steel skin doubler plate surrounding the muzzle of the NR-30 shows up clearly. The auxiliary spill door in the side of the nose opens at Mach numbers above 1.5 (later versions, 1.35) at anything less than maximum rpm*

grossly overstated the size, weight and engine thrust, and then, once actual figures were known in 1963, tend either to regard the aircraft as one of the greatest fighters of all time or as an aircraft so limited as to be virtually useless. It also helps if we can escape from the morass of confusing 'Fishbeds', but of course we have yet to encounter most of the puzzling suffix letters.

Where the original Type 74 aircraft is concerned, with Service designation MiG-21F-12 and F-13, the final result is an extraordinary mixture which just escapes *both* the above assessments! Use of a single R-11F-300 engine absolutely denied the aircraft the chance of a ratio of thrust to weight better than about 0.65, and this underlies most of the shortcomings. Typical F-series aircraft had an internal fuel capacity of only 2470 litres of which 2340 (515 Imp gal) were usable. Later versions have greater total capacity but even less usable fuel, as explained in subsequent chapters. This fuel capacity makes it difficult if not impossible to achieve the brochure performance. An Egyptian pilot told the author 'I know only one of my friends who has reached Mach 2, and he did that in an unauthorized dive'. In 1975 an Indian told *Flight*

*International* 'Few of my friends managed to accelerate to more than Mach 1.9 before the fuel ran short, and the absolute ceiling, which was nominally 60,000 ft (18,300 m), proved to be around 46,000 ft (14,020 m) even after following the climb/accelerate/dive/zoom procedure'. This very experienced Indian rated the MiG-21F as 'extremely poor' above 20,000 ft (6100 m), and said the Russians seemed happy to concentrate on low-level combat and ground attack.

Yet when the MiG-21 was being designed ground attack was entirely secondary, and the whole emphasis was put on flight performance, and especially air combat performance, at all altitudes. Somewhere in development, despite modest increases in engine thrust, the desired flashing performance was clearly lost. Part of the trouble was certainly an overweight airframe, though usually the MiG OKB has been good at weight estimation. When one considers the excellent dogfight performance of the Hunter, with a giant tray of four 30 mm cannon, each with more ammunition than the single gun of the MiG-21F, and on an engine of barely half the thrust and with a very much bigger airframe, the critical

weight problem of the MiG is hard to comprehend. And the MiG-21F would have roughly similar performance to that later version. The real problem, not only in the F but in later versions also, has been on takeoff. Landing, despite its high speed, has never been any problem. Indeed the reason for forbidding full-flap landings in nearly all versions was that on first depressing the flaps fully the aircraft 'balloons' severely, gaining perhaps 200 ft (60 m), whereupon the immediate reaction is to stuff the nose down. This comes just as speed bleeds off

LEFT
*A pilot of the CL (Czech air force) wearing bonedome and normal flying overalls. AOA and yaw vanes on the nose boom indicate that this aircraft is fitted with a gyro gunsight*

ABOVE
*Though often seen, this is an excellent picture of Soviet Frontal Aviation F-13s on a runway made of concrete hexagons with pitch-filled joints*

MiG-21Fs of the Czech CL undergoing line maintenance.
Nose booms are hinged up, some AOA/yaw vanes being
protected by drums. Some aircraft have glazed cockpit rear
fairings, unusual on Czech-built examples

BELOW
A standard Czech MiG-21F fitted with K-13 missile rails,
and with SRO-2 IFF beneath the cockpit

ABOVE
A MiG-21F-13 of the East German LSK is now on view
in the Armed Forces Museum in Dresden. No 1801 has a
drop tank and two DDR-type 16-57 rocket launchers
(R Vornholz via Robert J Ruffle)

OVERLEAF
A Hungarian MiG-21F-13, with a fuel bowser just
beyond, is marshalled out of a lineup. Ground crew are
assisting pilots in the other cockpits
(Interfoto MTI)

TOP LEFT
*MIG-21F-13s of the Yugoslav air force undergoing line maintenance. Full serial numbers are 22510, 22512 etc (L + K, via Robert J Ruffle)*

LEFT
*An F-13 of the East German LSK making a typical landing with only partial flap. The pilot has already streamed the drag chute and the cable is free (Flug Revue)*

ABOVE
*Another F-13 of the East German LSK, with K-13 rails (US Navy via Robert F Dorr)*

fast and the aircraft begins to sink uncontrollably, and a lot of MiG-21s were lost in full-flap landings in the early days. On takeoff, however, performance is marginal. It is mandatory to use at least half afterburner, though using any more eats into the very restricted fuel supply.

Almost all pilots of early MiG-21s, even those few who had Western fighter experience, praised the overall viceless behaviour and all-round manoeuvrability. They liked the view from the cockpit, which in the early MiG-21 versions rivalled that of the later and much more sophisticated F-16. The ejection of the canopy with the seat worked satisfactorily on most occasions, but not on others. The author naturally found MiG-21 pilots reticent about such matters, but both Indians and Egyptians were

ABOVE
*A Yugoslav F-13 in typical landing attitude, with forward airbrakes open. K-13 missiles are carried; without interface shoe each weighs 154 lb (70 kg)*
*(US Navy)*

LEFT
*Full rudder also brings in differential wheel brakes to swing Finnish* Ilmavoimat *(air force) No 78 on to the apron at Kuopio-Rissala. The Finnish Fs have all been replaced by the MiG-21bis*
*(MAP via Robert J Ruffle)*

prepared to comment that the 21F seat/canopy system was less than perfect. It certainly had no zero/zero capability (ie, it could not be used safely at rest on the ground) and all the evidence suggests that it had undesirably low limitations in safe escape G limits and IAS. Most pilots found the cockpit quite comfortable, though the canopy fitted rather closely round the pilot's helmet.

Though all flight-control surfaces were fully powered, every pilot spoken to by the author

considered the stick forces heavy, or even 'very heavy'. This is par for the course with Soviet fighters. Like the Su-7 family, the early MiG-21 was considered to be a beautiful aircraft to fly provided you were fit and strong! It was certainly an excellent aircraft for a 30-minute workout at low level on a fine day, especially flying 'by the seat of the pants'. Under these conditions there were no Mach or G limitations, though Soviet MiG-21 instructors prohibited rates of roll exceeding 90°/sec. Yet, rather curiously (because it is difficult to see a reason), the MiG-21F was almost crippled as a fighter by limitations in instrumentation.

Lack of a yaw damper or yaw autostab appears to have been no problem, and in any case Mach number very seldom exceeded unity on typical sorties. Later versions introduced automatic adjustment of the tailplane circuit according to IAS, but the 21F was originally equipped with a choice of two gear ratios manually selected by the pilot. A complex panel instrument displayed Mach and altitude, and indicated when to change from one tailplane regime to the other. This was not popular, partly because it

was an extra thing to remember in a mock (or real) dogfight but chiefly because one had to think ahead and decide how far the excursion into the alternative regime was likely to be permanent. More serious was the fact that the big black/white horizon was non-toppling in roll only. In a loop it locked near the top and then took some time to reset. This serious shortcoming was the fault of the panel instrument itself, because it was driven from a remote platform whose gyro was non-toppling about all axes.

Much skill is needed in designing a fighter cockpit. The early MiG-21s were adequate, but would never have been accepted by Western air forces. In some ways they resembled US fighters of World War 2 in that a large number of dial instruments were put wherever there was a convenient place, without any attempt to conform to a standardized overall layout. The scene was dominated by the giant central stick, which was taller than ideal—and needed to be,

ABOVE
*Two of the late-model MiG-21Fs imported into India, with small modifications including VHF radio with a blade aerial midway along the spine. Serials are BC816 and BC821*

UPPER RIGHT
*Like that on this page, this photograph of Indian Air Force BC821 was taken 'under combat conditions', probably on the Western Front with Pakistan. Even these early aircraft had operative S-3M radar warning (Indian Armed Forces Info Office)*

RIGHT
*This MiG-21F of the Indonesian AURI (air force) is in landing attitude. The angle was reduced, and pilot view ahead improved, by fitting SPS flaps*

TOP
*A revealing view of the Iraqi AF MiG, No 534, that defected to Israel on 16 August 1966. Note the flaps fully extended, and the braking parachute stuffed back in its open compartment under the rear fuselage*

ABOVE
*The same aircraft after its metamorphosis as '007' of Israel's Chel Ha'Avir (air force). All stencilling and labels, previously in English, were re-applied in Hebrew, and a new radio was fitted. Decor was red
(Robert J Ruffle archives)*

התקיף 14 ביולי 1966

1. לפני הפגיעה

2. הפגיעה

3. אחרי הפגיעה

ABOVE
*An exceptionally clear set of combat ciné frames showing cannon strikes on the left wing of a United Arab AF MiG-21F, which bursts into flames. The date (top) does not tally with a published Israeli victory*

because of the large forces needed. Beyond were instruments which were mostly far below the level of the pilot's eyes, so that accurate needle readings were often prevented by parallax errors. On the other hand, the pilot seldom needs a really accurate reading, and the acid test is that the system worked. It is difficult in these days of beautifully designed cockpits with Hotas (hands on throttle and stick) controls to assess the early MiG-21 fairly. By modern standards the pilot had to spend far too much time with his head down, looking 'into the office', but so he did with contemporary Western fighters.

Early MiG-21F fighters had unbelievably primitive armament. Many, including all early exports outside the Warsaw Pact, had no IFF and only limited radio. The gunsight was a plain fixed-reticle (graticule) type, a scarcely believable fact because from before 1950 the MiG-15 had been fitted with a gyro sight copied from the British Ferranti type. The MiG-21F-13 did have a gyro sight, giving the correct aim-off in deflection shooting against a turning target, yet according to pilots of customer air forces this used to topple at 2.75G. In the author's view it is unlikely to be the 2.75G acceleration in the vertical plane but the rate of turn that the sight cannot accommodate. Either way, this was another shortcoming of staggering proportions that is hard to explain, and it severely restricted dogfight capability. Discussing the problem with an Egyptian, the author formed the opinion that the almost useless sight was installed on aircraft armed with K-13As, which were not expected to use the gun at all. Actual use of the offset NR-30 caused noticeable yaw to the right, which was easily corrected by rudder, but does not appear to have interfered with engine operation (unlike the case on Soviet-built MiG-19s).

The only armament-related engine problem commonly experienced with the MiG-21 is flameout when firing salvos of rockets. This appears to affect later versions more than the MiG-21F, and in Egypt, for example, this problem is unknown on the early versions. Many pilots of the 21F have never dropped bombs, but those that have done so report no problem. Aiming is vaguely done with the gunsight in a dive of about 30°. One pilot told the author 'The best thing about the MiG-21F armament is how easily it can be rearmed on the ground. I once saw my aircraft given two M-62 bombs and a fresh load of 30 mm ammunition in seven minutes, and the tanks were topped up as well'.

Thus the early MiG-21F variants emerge as tough and simple machines which anyone can maintain in primitive conditions, and which a strong pilot can pole round the sky enjoyably, but which offers extremely limited weapons capability and that only in good visual conditions. The only situation in which a kill might reasonably be expected is when firing from behind on a target trying to get away in afterburner, when the K-13A emulates its US prototype in locking-on and staying locked-on.

# Chapter 5
# The Ye-7 family

As the MiG-21F was the basic series-produced member of the entire MiG-21F species it is the only version to be described here in detail. All other variants stem from it, and—apart perhaps from the Spitfire—no other combat aircraft in history has ever been subjected to so much development, through so many widely differing models, and over so long a period. One high-ranking Soviet pilot told the author 'The later ones are so different they might have been designated the MiG-42 or MiG-63, because they are about two or three times as useful'.

Certainly, the original 21F was one of the most limited fighters of the entire jet age. Back in the early 1960s Indians called it 'Our supersonic sports plane', though this was said in the nicest possible way. The enormous staff in Moscow concerned with Soviet military exports—nothing to do with Aviaexport, which handles purely civilian sales—were keenly aware of this, but not embarassed. They were able to offer a next-generation aircraft, and it was solely because of this that this very important export contract was concluded at all. The IAF would never have bought the MiG-21F-13 except as an interim advanced trainer for a better aircraft.

As explained, the original MiG-21 was a most carefully planned compromise. Korean experience dictated what Yakovlev had always preached, that fighters should be small and light. The IA-PVO, with their long runways, geographically vast operating regions and stand-off kill techniques, could afford to use very big, heavy and somewhat un-agile interceptors. Frontal Aviation, however, wanted fighters that could use front-line airstrips and outfly the enemy. It was widely known—Mikoyan himself confirmed the influence it exerted—that top USAF aces in Korea had said they would sacrifice anything, even items that seemed essential, such as an ejection seat, fuel and weapons, in order to outfly the enemy. Soviet pilots did not need to make such comments,

because the one thing the lightweight MiG-15 had to offer, apart from heavy guns, was superior climb and ceiling. It is ironic that it should have been this American pilot opinion that so strongly kept down the weight of the early MiG-21.

As early as 1956 the MiG OKB had schemed a Ye-6 with radar, but it seemed a pipe-dream. There was no official requirement, and preliminary calculations suggested that the CG (centre of gravity) position would be unacceptably far forward, and that weight and drag would result in too much degradation of performance for the small engine. The Tumanskii engine KB was heavily committed to solving immediate problems and in planning bigger engines for other fighters, such as the MiG-25, and it was only after 1957 that it recognized that, in the MiG-21, there was an application that might need a long series of R-11 developments.

Authorization for a major development of the Ye-6 series, carrying radar, was probably given in late 1957. By this time the MiG OKB was committed to Mach 2 interceptors with full radar (see Chapter 11) and to prove the nose geometry an aerodynamic prototype was flying before the end of that year. Downstream of the new nose this research aircraft, the SM-12PM, was basically an uprated MiG-19PM. A little later, in 1958, the SM-12PMU with a large booster rocket pack, took the 'big' radar and inlet system to speeds and heights beyond those anticipated for future MiG-21s.

There is little on record suggesting that the MiG OKB had any particular trouble with the new nose. This was in sharp contrast to the rival Sukhoi OKB, which agonized over how to put radar in the nose of a

*A fine portrait of a MiG-21FL, (with VVS individual number 69 in blue), on a visit to Swedish wing F16 at Uppsala in August 1967. Note the relocated braking parachute, and the ejection-seat top safety lever, armed by closing the canopy on it*
*(Claus Haugebo via Robert J Ruffle)*

*There is no reason to doubt that this, No 22, was anything other than a series PF, armed with two K-13 missiles only. Note the large dielectric fin-cap*

ABOVE
*The central aircraft, labelled 'trainer', is an early narrow-fin prototype used by the MiG OKB for tests on inlet systems. It was once used for propoganda pictures of 'training North Vietnamese pilots'*

*Very unusually this PFM has flaps at the maximum setting. It bears the 'standard of excellence' badge, and has been retrofitted with a rear-view mirror (Robert J Ruffle)*

fighter for six years (1954–60). Later, in a list of 'firsts', Sukhoi claimed to have perfected the design of a variable-geometry supersonic inlet containing radar. Mikoyan did not dispute this, though he argued about some of the others. Of course, a major part was played by the 'back room' engineers at TsAGI, which had given both design teams the basic shapes of their aircraft in the first place. It does seem, however, that it was Sukhoi that worked closer with the radar designers to come up with the best nose installation. This was because he had to. While the MiG management merely wished to offer competition, Sukhoi was under contract to develop his T-3 prototype (virtually a MiG-21 on a larger scale, with an engine of about twice the power) into an all-weather interceptor for the IA-PVO. He needed an amazing assortment of contrasting prototypes getting the nose right, some being illustrated in the author's *Aircraft of the Soviet Union*, also published by Osprey.

In any case it was easier with the 'big' interceptors because their inlets were sized to a mass flow of some 105 kg/s, compared with a mere 57 kg for the MiG-21. In order to accommodate even a small radar the MiG-21 inlet had to be totally redesigned. It was not possible merely to repeat the front end of the SM-12 prototypes because these had likewise been designed for much greater airflow, being twin-engined. Unlike

Sukhoi, the MiG team did not play about with odd arrangements but merely enlarged the MiG-21 inlet lip diameter from 690 mm to 910 mm, whilst rearranging the inner profile to handle the small mass flow required by the R-11F engine. It was recognized that this redesigned inlet automatically opened the way to future modification to pass greater airflows for possible future versions with more powerful engines, and in due course this was to prove very important.

The intake diagram shown on page 37 explains the aerodynamics. Such inlets are named for Oswatitsch, who 50 years ago explained how a conical centrebody can be made more efficient. If its angle increases (ideally in a smooth curve, but in practice usually in a series of steps) it generates the usual inclined shockwave at the tip as soon as the flight Mach number exceeds unity, and it also throws off weaker inclined shocks at each change in angle. Each shock is at a coarser angle, and they all focus in a ring some way off the surface of the cone. This intersection would normally result in an intense shock front coming inwards from that point, causing high drag, but the trick found by Oswatitsch is to put the sharp outer lip of the inlet a few millimetres in front of the focus. This eliminates the intense shock and inserts a weaker normal shock (one at right angles to the airflow), downstream of which the flow is subsonic.

*Surely the biggest of all Oswatitsch ogival conical centrebodies was that fitted to the mighty inlet of the recordbreaking MiG Ye-166, which is referred to in later chapters*

*Aircraft 62 of a Frontal Aviation regiment makes its characteristically firm landing, with partial flap and airbrakes open. Note the amount of hardware blocking the pilot's view ahead*

There are of course still problems to be solved in designing a practical inlet. One is that the inclined shockwaves generated by the conical centrebody inevitably try to separate the boundary layer (the airflow very close to the metal surface), which, unless the designer is very clever, results in most of the cone being covered in a shroud of violently turbulent air. This not only cuts down the effective area of the inlet through which air can flow into the engine but it also carries on downstream and enters the engine. This immediately destroys smooth flow through the inner part of the compressor, and tends to make the compressor stall, which results in bangs, pops, loss of thrust, possibly a flameout and in severe cases a wrecked engine. Less severe consequences result from the need to match intake geometry to Mach number, as explained earlier, but this becomes difficult when the centrebody contains a full-blown search radar. MiG's answer was the same as Sukhoi's, in that the cone, made of glassfibre to serve as a radome transparent to the radar signals, translates around the non-sliding aerial (US = antenna). The inlet control system is almost the same as in the MiG-21F, but instead of having three preselected positions the cone can slide evenly to any location. Moreover, the problem of turbulence in the boundary layer is tackled quite differently. Instead of merely adding vortex generators the entire boundary layer is sucked out through a slit surrounding the translating cone. This slit remains approximately the same in all flight conditions, and the air removed is sucked out through ducts above and below leading to prominent aft-facing exits. The exits create the suction; no attempt was made to generate useful thrust.

The inlet duct downstream was unchanged, and the spill doors remained. The only other significant alterations at the front were to add provision for SRO-2 (later -2M) IFF aerials on the underside of the nose, either in front of or behind the nose gear, to cover the lower hemisphere, and to relocate the pitot boom above the nose. In its lower position the boom had been a nuisance; not being as massive as that on Su aircraft, it was easily damaged, and was often folded upwards. It was not unknown for pilots to scramble with it in that position, and at least this was no longer possible with the boom rigidly fixed above the inlet. At first, and throughout PF production, it was on the centreline. Pilots liked the boom in that position as a rough index of attitude and drift.

Another problem to which the MiG engineers addressed themselves was how to operate from rough airstrips. Almost everything necessary had been done before. The OKB had plenty of experience with low-pressure tyres, a.t.o. (assisted takeoff) rockets and

ABOVE
*The structures department at the MAI (Moscow Aviation Technical Institute in 1973. In the foreground is what is almost certainly the MiG-21DPD. Beyond are the Yak-32 fuselage and a curiously modified Su-15*
*(Robert J Ruffle archives)*

ABOVE
*Another landing shot, this time by a Polish PF whose pilot is so far back he cannot be seen. Main landing-gear legs are appreciably longer when not under load*

BELOW
*Another Polish PF, with centreline tank and wing K-13 pylons. The radome boundary-layer upper overboard exit is seen clearly from this angle*

various forms of arrester gear. Back in 1956 trials had been flown with five SM-30s, aircraft in the MiG-19 family which were fired at 300 km/h from a steeply inclined mobile launch ramp (modified from a coastal cruise-missile system) and recovered by a cable arrester system which owed something to French work. Suffice to say not only did this not go into service but it was not considered for the MiG-21.

There was little difficulty in fitting a.t.o. rockets. The OKB had played with such things often, and it was almost a routine task selecting the correct solid motors, with canted nozzles, and designing the attachment interface unit. The latter, not part of either the motor or the aircraft, picks up on the main-spar fuselage frame under the wing on each side, with a rear steadying attachment on the main engine mounting frame. With a.t.o. fired the acceleration is typically 1.8G, and the wheels can leave the ground in about 150 m.

So far as the author knows no attempt was made to try cable arrester systems with the MiG-21, but it was certainly felt that the original braking parachute installation left much to be desired. Accordingly a completely new parachute (not the OKB's responsibility) and installation were designed. The new canopy is a cruciform design, only 29 per cent greater in deployed diameter—or rather, span—than the original circular pattern but offering approximately twice the retardation when deployed. It is easier to pack, the four arms rolling up into a tight cylinder which is then loaded into a new tubular housing between the jetpipe and rudder. The container is closed by twin spring-loaded doors, through which the canopy is positively expelled, opening automatically within 1.5 seconds.

Introduction of the improved drag chute was delayed until after 1965, though service trials took place with one of the Ye-6T development prototypes of the original MiG-21F as early as 1959. (The same aircraft carried out some of the first trials with a.t.o. rockets.) Another feature not introduced at once was the fitting of larger wheels and tyres. This was needed to match tyre pressure to the bearing strength specified for front-line airstrips, and the MiG designers decided to try to do a little better still, to allow for likely further growth in gross weight. Some years earlier the Poles had rigged up a soft-field version of their licensed MiG-17F with tandem-wheel main gears retracting into grotesque forward wing-root extensions. Mikoyan himself thought this 'a case of letting the tactical demand destroy the basic concept'. With the MiG-21 even the original main wheels had necessitated small blisters above and below the wing, and the simple answer seemed to be to fit bigger wheels and bigger blisters. From the viewpoint of the Area Rule the larger bulges could hardly have come at a worse place, but the difference in speed was extremely small. The 800-mm tyres could make the mandatory 'firm landings' with the new aircraft at pressures down to 0.7 MPa, but the

pressure written into the manual was 0.785, or 115 lb/sq in, a reduction of almost one-quarter over that of the lighter MiG-21F. The larger wheels lie at a slight angle from the vertical in the fuselage, having rotated 87° on the ends of their legs.

Last of the major changes made with the Ye-7 prototypes was to redesign the cockpit canopy. When asked about this, Mikoyan said the reason was simply to reduce drag, but in view of the exhaustive nature of tunnel work at TsAGI before ever the Ye-2 and Ye-5 were built, one wonders that anything could have been wrong in the first place. The changes were not important, but, together with the larger nose, they completely altered the appearance of the aircraft. The canopy was restressed, and the hinge was redesigned so that the canopy was hinged direct to a fuselage frame, the previous small fixed portion under the windshield being eliminated. The canopy frame was revised, and the fairing downstream was enlarged so that it curved back from the canopy to meet the original profile at a sudden change in profile at the main wing front-spar frame.

This increase in internal volume enabled internal fuel capacity to be increased. The main UKV and RSIU communications boxes were raised into the new fairing, enabling the forward tank to be increased in size, raising total system capacity from 2340 (usable) to 2850 litres. In practice, according to pilots, the extra capacity could not all be used, because when internal fuel has fallen to 800 litres the CG has moved so far aft that the aircraft becomes unflyable, pitching uncontrollably nose-up if speed is allowed to bleed off.

This completes the main changes introduced in the first Ye-7, flown in early 1959. At this time the Sapphire radar was not quite ready and it was replaced by ballast. The engine remained the R11F-300, and armament continued to be provision for two NR-30 guns, only the right-hand gun being installed. At about this time, doubtless after long debate about the value of such weapons, the decision was taken to remove all provision for guns, leaving two K-13A AAMs or launchers for 57 mm rockets as the sole armament. This was not an easy decision to take, but it countered the increased fuel mass and also enabled the twin forward airbrakes to be made simpler and more effective. On almost any basis the armament must be judged inadequate.

In 1959 the Sapphire radar was delivered to the OKB for trial installation, another having reached the Su team a few weeks earlier. A simple set using thermionic valves (vacuum tubes) and with peak power of about 100 kW, it is also known as the RP-9 and R1L. The aerial (antenna) is a plain circular parabolic dish with the waveguide feeding backwards from the focus to the reflector. The dish scans conically, spinning about an axis pointing dead ahead (NATO later called this set Spin Scan). In the search mode it operates at PRFs (pulse repetition frequencies) of 825–950 Hz, covering a forward sector 30° to either side and 15° to above and below. The pilot display is a simple CRT forming part of the ASP-PF sight system. Modern bright phosphors were not available, so the display was fitted with a visor to permit daylight viewing. It was the first time a bulky visor had appeared in the cockpit of a Frontal Aviation aircraft, though of course such things had long been common in the IA-PVO.

Learning about radar was a major task for over 20,000 pilots and a much greater number of ground personnel. The diagrams on page 66 show the R1L presentation in the search and firing (literally 'taking aim') modes. By modern standards the Sapphire radar is archaic, but in the context of its time and environment it marked a very large step-forward. In the tracking mode PRF jumps to 1,750–1,850 Hz. The rectilinear graticule vanishes, and the pilot flies to keep the short horizontal line that represents the target inside the aiming ring. He then has to close the range, shown by the vertical 'PUSK' scale on the right, until he can fire one of the SRs (self-guided rockets). An overt copy of the American AIM-9B Sidewinder, the K-13A 'SR' also was later developed to have the original's aural signal in the pilot's headset, starting with a growl once the target has been sighted by the homing head, and changing to an urgent singing when fully locked-on at close range. At the same time it was, like AIM-9B, good only for attacks from astern against full-throttle targets, and erratic even then.

Effective range of the Sapphire is about 20 km in good conditions, with a bomber target, closing to only about 8 km before switching to the 'taking aim' mode. As the diagrams show, in the search mode the main display shows the target in a box between two horizontal lines whose separation is proportional to target range. The vertical scale on the right contains a bright 'blip' indicating target elevation, while beneath the main display are numeric readouts of target height and range, both in km, and the time remaining before AAM firing (0.6 minutes in the example given).

There is often a sharp contrast between the performance of senior OKB test pilots and that of inexperienced pilots, who in the Soviet Union can include young conscripts. There have been several cases where Soviet test pilots have found nothing wrong with aircraft that the front-line regiments either could not handle at all or suffered an unacceptable level of casualties. So far as is known this was never the case with the MiG-21, though all sorts of problems did occur. Pilots on conversion to the F version were known to overshoot or even collide with target aircraft, or run out of fuel, all because they had their eyes glued to the ASP-PF scope and were concentrating to the exclusion of all else. On the whole, however, the Ye-7 development into the production Type 76 was judged a considerable success. The only retrograde steps were slight degradation of rearward vision and loss of gun

A September 1966 portrait of Marina Solovyeva, who on the 16th of that month set a world 500-km closed-circuit record at 2062 km/h, beating Jacqueline Cochran's existing mark by a wide margin. Aircraft, Ye-76
(Tass)

armament. It must be remembered that 1960 was a time when all the signals coming back from the USA and Britain were that guns were obsolete; indeed the RAF professed to think that *all combat aircraft* were obsolete.

By the time the Type 76 got into production it was the winter 1960–61, and a further small change to its appearance was to move the VHF radio back along the dorsal spine together with its slightly sweptback rigid blade aerial. Early Type 76s also retained the original braking-parachute installation, possibly because of delay in delivering the outstanding new design of parachute canopy. Service designation of the Type 76 was intended to be MiG-21P, for *perekhvatchik*, interceptor, but before the start of production the uprated R-11F2-300 version of the original engine passed its qualification tests and was immediately adopted. Almost installationally identical to the F-300, the new engine had an enlarged afterburner giving increased maximum thrust at all

*Informal portrait of Lydia Zaitseva, who on 23 June 1965 held an altitude of 19,020 m in a MiG-21UM and on 28 March 1967 covered a 1000-km circuit in the Ye-76 at 1298 km/h*
*( Norvosti)*

TOP
*Yevginia Martova is seen here (at foot of steps, nearer to camera) when serving as copilot on a recordbreaking Il-62M of Aeroflot*
*( Tass)*

RIGHT
*A contrasting picture of Lydia Zaitseva, fully kitted up for her Ye-76 mission. By profession she is a flying instructor with DOSAAF*
*( Novosti)*

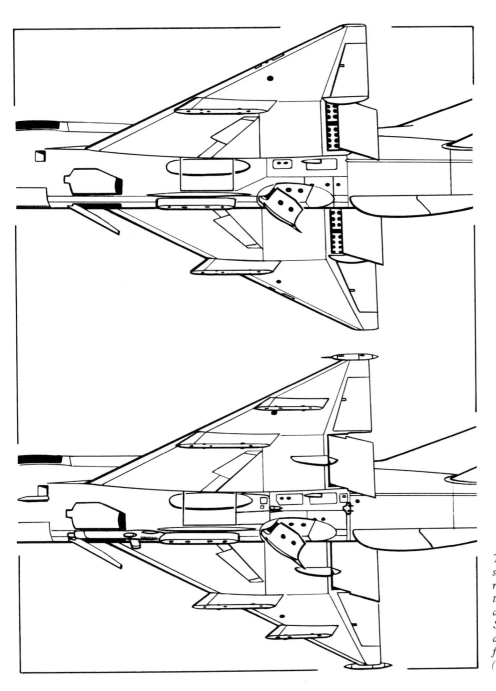

*The original track-mounted slotted flap (in some ways resembling the Fowler) travelled aft and down on attachments at the tips. The SPS (lower) is simply hinged at mid-span. Note RWR tip fairings on the SPS aircraft (Pilot Press)*

altitudes (see Appendix 1). With the F2-300 engine the new fighter became the MiG-21PF, F for boosted.

One Ye-76, bearing number 22, was used much later by women pilots to set FAI-confirmed records. On 16 September 1966 Marina Solovyeva flew a 500-km circuit at 2062 km/h. On 11 October 1966 Yevgenia Martova flew a 2000-km circuit at 900.267 km/h. On 18 February 1967 Martova flew round a tight 100-km circuit at 2128.7 km/h. On 28 March 1967 Lydia Zaitseva covered a 1000-km circuit at 1298.16 km/h. Obviously the 100 and 500-km circuits, the latter taking 15 minutes, were flown with full afterburner; some MiG-21 drivers would love to learn how it was done.

Chronologically the next significant development was the introduction of blown flaps. The Attinello flap, in which very hot high-pressure air bled from the main engine is blasted at supersonic speed in a thin sheet over the top of the flap, had been tested on a Grumman F9F back in 1953. Subsequently it had been used on production aircraft, beginning with the Lockheed F-104, but it was its use on the F-4 Phantom II that made TsAGI take keener interest because this showed that it could be used to improve a large wing rather than make possible a small one. TsAGI had carried out its first blown-flap experiments, with various jet aircraft, from 1957. To a first-order approximation the Institute found that, if a normal high-speed wing could reach a lift coefficient of 2 with an area-increasing slotted flap, then a value of 3 could be attained with good blown flaps. Called SPS (*sduva pogranichnovo sloya*), blown flaps were designed by the MiG OKB for the MiG-21, and studied for other types, notably the Ye-266 (later MiG-25), but not adopted on those aircraft.

For the MiG-21 there was just enough air-bleed capability from the R-11F2-300 to make it worth while. Of course a basic drawback is that it is impossible to use flap blowing and still get full engine thrust. Careful control must be exercised to ensure that extracting the enormous bleed flow does not result in turbine inlet temperature going 'off the clock'. Excessive temperature, or a demand for more thrust, automatically means less flap-blowing, and this in turn means a sudden loss in lift. With the SPS system of the Ye-7SPS, flown in 1961, the bleed pipes go straight from the large connections on each side of the combustion-chamber casing to the wing-root spars on each side, and thence along the front of each flap to terminate in a fishtail pipe very similar to that used in Western flap-blowing systems. The flaps themselves are of slightly greater chord than the original pattern. Instead of running out and down on tracks at each end they are simply hinged, pulled down by a hydraulic actuator at the flap mid-span point. The prominent actuator fairing immediately shows the presence of SPS flaps.

The actuators are served by the basic duplicated hydraulic system with a pressure of 20.59 MPa, and the forces involved are considerable as the flap is driven from a point only a few inches from the hinge. The actuator is not irreversible, but even at full hydraulic pressure allows the flap to bleed off progressively as speed is increased beyond 400 km/h (248 mph), the flaps being forced fully up at about 700 km/h (435 mph). Like almost everything about the MiG-21 this cuts both ways. It facilitates use of flap in air combat, a technique first used by the Pakistanis with the Chinese F-6 and then exploited with some success by the Egyptians in October 1973. A pilot can select full flap and then pull G in 'full burner' knowing that the flaps will reduce his turn radius without greatly affecting speeds and longitudinal accelerations. On the other hand the flaps do keep sapping at the energy state, and most Western fighter pilots would never accept such a situation. All this presupposes that the flaps fold back against air loads symmetrically, which is by no means guaranteed. Even in their normal use on landing the flaps have qualities that might not be acceptable to Western nations. Even more than with the original tracked unblown flaps the SPS causes the MiG-21 first to 'balloon' violently upwards, immediately followed by rapid loss of speed and dramatic rate of sink. The Russians teach firm, almost no-flare, landings, but use of full flap is normally forbidden because the sink rate is excessive. Only the most experienced MiG-21 pilots are permitted to practise full-flap landings,

using a lot of stick and throttle to minimize the initial ballooning and then keep up airspeed and get established at an acceptable rate of descent. Visiting MiG-21 units from Frontal Aviation in Sweden and France have landed at the same partial flap setting as used for takeoff.

Though the F2S engine was installationally almost unchanged, apart from the bleed pipes, the aperture at the rear of the fuselage, closely surrounding the variable afterburner nozzle, has from 1966 been stiffened by welding and riveting an extra strip of high-nickel alloy round the top and bottom. This gives the end of the fuselage a slightly kinked appearance when seen from the side.

The MiG-21PF reached FA regiments in 1963, by which time it had already given way to much later versions on the MiG OKB drawing boards. However, from 1962 the Indian Air Force began to exert a wholly unexpected influence, and this was directed not so much at onward development as on the rectification of shortcomings. In the Soviet system, despite a long-term awareness of the problem, the rigid 'class' hierarchy has made it almost impossible to establish a proper feedback from front-line units to the design bureaux. Bureau leaders have commented on their surprise, on visiting combat units, to learn of serious problems (often causing casualties) of months' or years' standing. But the IAF evaluation pilots were able to discuss the MiG-21 objectively and report their unbiased findings, and these found their way to Mr Mikoyan himself almost immediately.

On the whole the PF, or rather a slightly simplified model for export known as the FL, was regarded by the Indians very highly indeed. They had never known an aircraft with such performance and manoeuvrability, and the engineering staff were impressed by its simplicity and easy maintenance. The engine TBO of 200 hours, soon to be raised to 250, was considered acceptable, and even the short life of many airframe and system parts was not thought a major problem. But the Indians were deeply concerned about the fundamental problem of limited carrying capacity, which translated into weak armament and short range. Summarized, the IAF wanted more fuel, guns and a gunsight, better brakes and better tyres.

Dealing with the simple matters first, the IAF was concerned at the high incidence of tyre bursts, and the generally short life of tyres at the Lugovaya training centre, and this was tackled by both the Soviets and the Indians designing superior multi-ply tyres using Western type methods and materials. In the IAF, at least, keeping tyres at full pressure also helped greatly in minimizing tyre heating during the long, high-speed ground runs, and even in operations from high-altitude airfields the IAF seldom has tyre-bursts. The pneumatic braking system was never really popular, but after enough effort had been put behind the complaint the Soviet section responsible

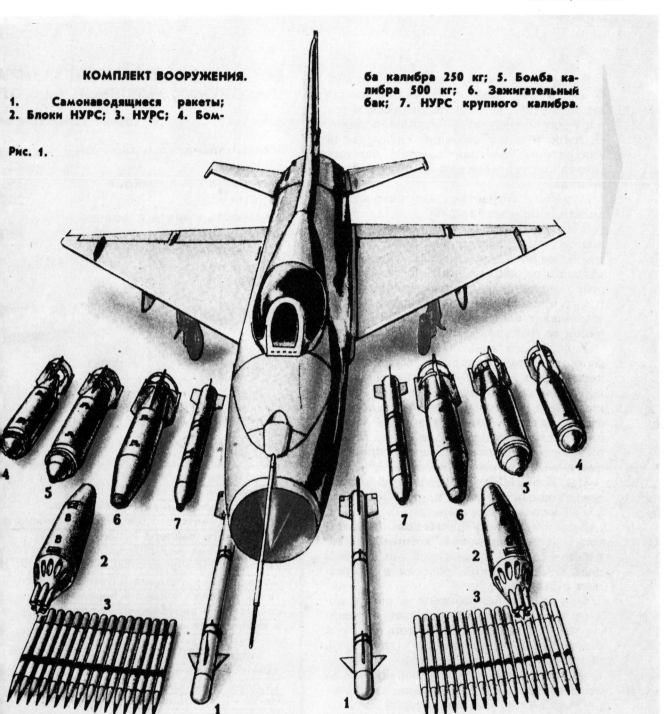

**КОМПЛЕКТ ВООРУЖЕНИЯ.**

1. Самонаводящиеся ракеты;
2. Блоки НУРС; 3. НУРС; 4. Бомба калибра 250 кг; 5. Бомба калибра 500 кг; 6. Зажигательный
бак; 7. НУРС крупного калибра.

Рис. 1.

*A helpful little sketch which actually shows a MiG-21F but could equally be a PF. Key: 1, K-13A; 2, UV-16-57; 3, 57-mm rockets; 4, FAB-250; 5, FAB-500; 6, tank; 7, S-240 heavy rocket*

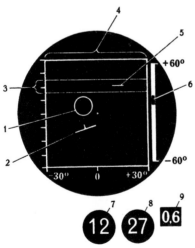

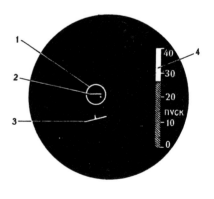

was persuaded to redesign the system to operate at greater pressure, with greater stored energy, until the limiting factors were overheating and pad life. Steering by differential braking has been retained on all subsequent models of MiG-21.

One of the modifications not called for by the Indians was a further increase in fin chord, achieved by a second forwards extension of the leading edge. This was flown on the original Ye-7 prototype, as a retroactive modification. The increase in root chord

TOP
*The first GP-9 gunpack, installed on a MiG-21FL (Type 77) of the Indian Air Force. The missile is a PK-13A*

ABOVE
*Sapphire aiming diagrams: 'search/track mode' (left) displays 1. aiming circle 2. spacial position of aircraft 3. proportional to target range 4. azimuth sector (60°) 5. target 6. strobe angle 7. target height (km) 8. target range (km) 9. time-to-launch/fire (minutes). 'Taking aim mode' at right displays 1. aiming angle 2. target 3. spacial position of aircraft 4. firing pointer for rocket/missile launch*

was no less than 470 mm (18.5 in), and it required an almost complete structural redesign of the fin. The main spar was more acutely swept, internal structure and skin stiffened, and the extremely broad top capped with an exceptionally large glassfibre moulding covering the VHF and UHF communications blades. A small flush plate aerial on each side serves the RSIU (very short wave fighter radio), while the top of the fin is projected aft above this rudder to house a navigation light, SRO-2M IFF, Sirena passive warning radar aerial, left/right formation-keeping lights and the fuel-system vent.

What was purely the result of discussions with the Indians was a major improvement in armament and fuel. There was no real prospect of increasing internal fuel capacity, but it was agreed that the export MiG-21FL should be to a new standard, Type 77, with the wing pylons plumbed for tanks. Thus the external fuel capacity was doubled. The reason it was not tripled was because the fuselage attachment was taken over by the GP-9 gondola containing a GSh-23L twin-barrel gun with 200 rounds of 23 mm ammunition. The gun was new, having been cleared for service only in 1959. Like all Soviet guns it is outstanding, weighing 72 kg and firing a 200 g projectile with muzzle velocity of 890 m/s at a cyclic rate of 2,800 per minute. With this came a predictor gunsight and a signal feed-in of target range from the modified (R2L) radar. Very little development flying was required, the gondola made little difference to speed or handling, and it was far enough from the nose to have little effect on engine behaviour. The first GP-9s and sights were supplied in crates to India where they were installed at IAF Base Repair Depots in 1965–6.

Addition of the GP-9 can fairly be described as the point at which the MiG-21 ceased to be a 'supersonic sports plane' and became an air combat fighter to be reckoned with. Soviet pilots seldom fire expensive missiles in training, and it may be that—as in the USA at this time—the effectiveness of early AAMs had been over-rated. Time after time in the December 1971 war with Pakistan, K-13A missiles failed to perform as advertised, just like the early Sidewinders in Vietnam. In contrast, the GSh-23L not only never failed to work but soon gained the first two victories of that war. It proved a tremendous morale-booster, and one can only feel enduring surprise at the inadequate armament which at that time was thought adequate by the Soviet Union. Today, for the record, the latest Frontal Aviation fighters carry not two missiles but eight.

With such a wealth of modifications appearing in quick succession it is small wonder that it has been difficult to keep track of designations. NATO hardly helped, by inventing a string of 'Fishbed' suffix letters which bore little relationship to chronological

sequence and in any case were flawed by errors. Some of the improvements appeared on particular models, only to be absent from later ones—usually for reasons of customer choice. India's Type 77 incorporated everything except Sirena 3 and SRO-2M, though the latter was granted a Soviet export licence in the 1970s. Otherwise the 77 featured SPS, broad fin, large wheels, new drag chute, improved brakes and tyres, and, of course, the GP-9 gondola and twin wing tanks. All this considerably increased maximum weight, but it was still possible to take off on half afterburner and land at 270 km/h provided the airfield was not far above sea level.

In the Soviet Union the SPS flaps were introduced on the PF(SPS) in 1963, and continued in winter 1964–5 with the broad-fin PFS. Soviet MiG-21s of these series did use the GP-9 gondola, but there is no evidence this was ever a widespread fit. Likewise NATO invented a Fishbed-E said to resemble the MiG-21F but with the latest broad fin, revised drag chute and GP-9 installation. No such aircraft existed, even the gun pack being tested in prototype form on a Ye-7 series development aircraft.

The MiG OKB flew a further prototype in the early 1960s designated Aircraft 75. The author has no information on this, though curiously there is some evidence that Type 75 has been associated with the 21bis, the ultimate MiG-21 of the 1970s.

Conversely, there is evidence that the last of the Ye-7 'PF' family, the PFM (PF *Modifikatsirovanii*), is the Type 94. This seems nonsense. The Soviet Union seldom goes out of its way to mislead with false designations, and most of its designations are supremely logical. In due course all may be revealed. Suffice to report that the PFM, which entered service in 1965, is a late-series PF with a new ejection seat and canopy.

Inability to use the SK seat at heights below 110 m (361 ft) had resulted in numerous fatalities by the mid-1960s, and in any case the unique departure of the interlinked seat and canopy had itself caused various problems and at least one fatality. After prolonged conferences the decision was taken to switch to a conventional arrangement with a side-hinged canopy and fixed windshield. This had the incidental advantage of improving birdstrike resistance, though it added a massive frame round the pilot's forward field of view which was already totally unacceptable by Western standards, the view ahead being discerned through chinks in the solid mass of visor, sight and high coaming.

The real improvement lay in the KM-1 seat, lighter and even more comfortable than the old K and with zero/zero performance. Though its use involves a routine with safety pins it is considered much less cumbersome than the previous overhead safety arm, and its reliability has proved to be excellent.

# Chapter 6
# Ye-7 family in service

As explained in Chapter 5, the Indian Air Force played a major role in influencing the MiG-21 programme. When the Indians bought the MiG-21F it was not only a shock to the West—and to Britain in particular, which had regarded India as a captive market—but also a slight shock to the Soviet Union. There has rarely been a more limited fighter than the MiG-21F, but on balance it was felt that its speed, good handling and general fine qualities made up for its limited range and endurance, lack of search radar and weak armament. By modern standards the armament of two AAMs seems unbelievably poor for a dedicated air combat fighter, but we must remember that it was just at this time (1962–63) that the RAF asked BAC to delete the two 30 mm guns from the next version of the Lightning, the F.3, leaving two missiles as the sole armament.

This was certainly a low point in fighter procurement. The marvellous new missiles had so captured the imagination of the policymakers that on the one hand they considered two of them adequate armament and, on the other, they instantly regarded the gun as 'old hat' and to be left off as soon as possible. It was widely believed that fighters would not need to close to visual range, the missiles killing automatically at distances of several miles. What had not been considered were such basic facts as the need to down more than two aircraft per sortie, the fact that a war might come along in which positive visual identification was a political prerequisite before opening fire, and, not least, that the missile might simply fail to work as advertised.

In August 1962, when the Indians signed the original agreement to purchase the MiG-21F, there was already a firm programme to update the aircraft, and it was this that tipped the balance in favour of the aircraft in the IAF purchase. It is thus rather surprising that so many of the F model were not only manufactured but also exported to countries outside the Warsaw Pact. Even stranger, many of these customers still fly the original F model in various sub-types, usually with no more than superficial updating over the past 20 years. The MiG OKB was never requested to devise a field kit for converting Fs into PFs or FLs, and no such conversions were ever carried out.

It is still far from clear precisely which model of the second generation was supplied to which countries, but the basic airframe is the Type 76 (PF) or 77 (FL). To make life harder at least some of the SPS aircraft are Type 76, though they are clearly later in development timing. Again, so far as the author can tell, the R2L differs only in details from the basic R1L and is merely an export version lacking features considered security-sensitive by the Soviet Union. Certainly the R2L was considered acceptable to the IAF, which however exerted strong pressure on the Soviet government to improve the MiG-21FL to increase its combat effectiveness. As mentioned earlier the improvements concerned brakes and tyres, internal fuel capacity, the sight and the weapon fit. The GP-9 gun gondola was already being tested in the Soviet Union, but the author believes this had not been intended for the MiG-21FL which had originally been planned as the final member of the PF

**LEFT**
*Soviet Frontal Aviation MiG-21PFs being serviced and refuelled by hand-held gravity hose just like a car. The hardstand seems somewhat littered*

**BELOW LEFT**
*Getting aboard a Soviet PF, using the usual free-standing type of ladder. Note that the instrument boom is at 'twelve o'clock' on this model*

**RIGHT**
*A Frontal Aviation FL seen at Uppsala, Sweden, in 1967. Note the new braking-parachute container*

**BELOW**
*This standard PF was displayed with a placard under the nose saying it was the Ye-66 (Robert J Ruffle archives)*

This PFM of Frontal Aviation looks every inch an
operational machine, even to having a.t.o. rockets attached,
yet it is being ministered to by curiously garbed civilians!
Note canopy stay rod
(Robert J Ruffle archives)

PRECEDING PAGES
Three Type 77 fighters of the Indian Air Force, with
two Type 66-400 trainers

ABOVE
This was the first Type 77 (MiG-21FL) to be completed
by Hindustan Aeronautics at Nasik. Most Indian single-
seaters have two red 'danger' triangles beside the cockpit.
Later many FLs were camouflaged
(Robert J Ruffle archives)

UPPER RIGHT
Going through the cockpit check prior to scrambling in an
Indian Type 77. Auxiliary inlet covers and the boarding
steps have to be removed

RIGHT
Touchdown by a Type 77. Though the aircraft is firmly
down the pilot has not yet deployed the braking parachute

(77) series with broader fin, relocated parachute and (according to some authorities) slightly more internal fuel. Few countries appear to use the GP-9 gondola other than the Soviet Union, India and Yugoslavia, though every MiG-21 operator uses the K-13 family of AAMs. Indeed the K-13A manufacturing licence accompanied the original Indian purchase of the MiG-21, together with a manufacturing licence for the MiG-21FL and the F2S engine.

This programme far transcended anything previously attempted in India, and the government formed a special organization, Aeronautics (India), to manage it. This later became the MiG Complex (officially the MiG Division) of Hindustan Aeronautics Ltd (HAL). With so big a programme the government was concerned to provide employment as a social service in depressed areas, despite the fact that this enormously complicated the management task. By 1963 two prime sites had been selected, both not only without an aircraft factory but also without skilled employees of any kind. The MiG airframe factory, assembly complex and flight-test airfield was established at Ozar, near Nasik, a major town about 100 miles north-east of Bombay. Here a totally new facility was gradually built up, peaking in the 1970s at about 7,800 personnel of whom about half had to be found HAL houses or flats. More difficult still, the F2S engine plant may seem almost to have been a social service that ulitimately happened to produce engines—and there could hardly be a more challenging example of high-technology engineering. The entire plant complex was built near Koraput, in Orissa, in the east of the country about 300 miles northeast of Hyderabad and 500 miles southwest of Calcutta. There was previously nothing there. A dirt road passed close by, there was a railway 50 miles to the east, and nothing else. All that had to be done was build a complex of factories, a town, and put in electric power, water, sewerage, schools, shops, police, transportation and everything else. And this was all in order to build the Tumanskii R-11F2S fighter engine!

By any reckoning, to get most of Nasik and Koraput not merely in being but in production by late 1965 was a miracle, and the first FL Type 77, with a Soviet engine, was handed over to the IAF in November 1966. Meanwhile, the MiG Complex directors under Air Commodore C R Kurpad had picked a third site, at Balanagar, near the great city of Hyderabad, to make not only the fighter's avionics but also the K-13A AAM. This factory group soon employed 1,700 engineers and 1,300 manual workers, and though it initially assembled Soviet hardware, it gradually built an increasing proportion in-house, so that by the 1970s even the R2L radar was more than half Indian-made, quite apart from being Indian-assembled. In the same way the engine began as an assembly job, with first delivery in March 1968, and progressed until only about 15 per cent was being imported from the Soviet Union.

Every visitor to HAL—except perhaps those from the Soviet Union—is left in no doubt that the company has a very high opinion indeed not only of the MiG-21 but also of Soviet methods in general. One unexpected comment is that the fighter uses roughly twice as many forgings and castings as contemporary Western fighters. Though the MiG is regarded by the IAF as a bit of a toy compared with the massive Su-7, imported at the same time, it shares the same robust approach, with a 200 per cent safety factor slapped on almost everything (indeed, hydraulic hoses can be tested at four times the design pressure of 3,000 lb/sq in). The engine is particularly

*A picture which really brings out the unique character of the Type 77 and other members of the Ye-7 family, which formed a major halfway house between the early Ye-6 fighters (such as the F) and the Ye-9s (such as the MF). Note the impressive 800-mm main tyres (Pilot Press)*

praised. The West harbours a basic belief that, the more advanced the technology, the greater the disparity between the Soviet Union and the Western nations. Yet the R-11F2S engine, designed originally in 1954–55 and improved to F2S form in 1959, exhibits almost all the features of today's Western fighter engines including two spools running in squeeze-film bearings with an overhung first stage with blading looking exactly like that of the latest Western turbofans, a compact annular combustor with high-capacity bleeds for flap-blowing, and an extremely good and compact afterburner with a multi-flap profiled nozzle, with instant afterburner light-up and smooth modulation of thrust up to the maximum. Koraput engineers, many of whom had learned their skills on Hunters and Canberras, tend to describe the R-11 as 'tough and reliable like an Avon, but much easier to make or repair and much more advanced in design'. In fact the engine is not unlike an advanced 200-series Avon in mass flow and power, but despite being more 'rugged' it is smaller and lighter.

Yet another HAL factory, Lucknow in the north, contributes a wide range of accessories for most of the on-board fluid systems and electric power, and also makes landing gears. The entire MiG programme was planned to build up in four stages to the maximum local content, tailored to a peak output of 30 aircraft per year. In fact this level was not quite attained, and for most of the time Nasik, in particular, has run at about one-third of full capacity. To some degree this is because the Soviet advisors were so used to manufacture at extremely high rates (such as 48 per month) that they got the Indians to build in a lot of overcapacity which has not been fully utilized. Anyone who knows India will also appreciate the social, labour and other problems, even in factories where virtually every worker lives on site in a company house. The sheer length of the supply line from Soviet sources has also been another problem, so the fairly steady output of extremely high-quality MiG-21s of three major successive generations is no small accomplishment.

The first of the Ye-7 family to reach India were two Type 76 (MiG-21PF) which arrived together with four of the original MiG-21Fs in June 1964. After very brief inspections and a few flights, mainly by test pilots and senior staff officers, they were assigned to the trials squadron, No 28, which was already experienced on the basic MiG-21 having been flying the 21F from April 1964. It had been planned to build up strength and licence manufacture with a rapid import of complete aircraft sent by ship from Odessa to Bombay, and of CKD (component knocked-down) kits for assembly as too ambitious, not least because the factories did not yet exist. Instead, it was planned to build up in the four stages mentioned previously. To begin with it was planned to ship in 18 Soviet-built PFs in 1965, followed by a batch of the definitive IAF Type 77 (FL) for assembly at Nasik under the

supervision of MiG engineers, who are used to doing exactly the same thing at each of the manufacturing plants in the Soviet Union assigned to produce aircraft of MiG design.

A substantial MiG team (about 35 is usual inside the Soviet Union) duly arrived at Nasik, and later a Tumanskii team arrived at Koraput. But the 18 aircraft did not arrive in 1965, because in September, just as the batch were about to be shipped, the simmering border dispute with Pakistan erupted into full-scale local war. Everyone was eager to see how the Soviet fighter would shape up in combat with the Pakistani F-104A Starfighters, but, despite the eight serviceable MiGs flying intensive CAPs over two forward airfields in the Punjab, no hostile aircraft were encountered. Late in the year a small batch of

trainers arrived (the MiG-21U family are discussed in a separate chapter), and it was 1966 before complete and CKD aircraft began to arrive in earnest. The first FL assembled at Nasik from imported components, and with a Soviet-built engine, was handed over in early 1967; this was late, but in the author's view was still a commendable achievement. From then on Nasik and its supplier plants gradually introduced local materials and parts of local manufacture, and on 2 January 1969 Koraput at last delivered its first F2S engine. Then in a ceremony on 19 October 1970 the IAF accepted Type 77 number C1100, the first to be built from the definitive total (of just over 60 per cent) of local materials and parts. The Type 77 programme was completed at the 196th aircraft in January 1973.

One of the major items never made in India was the GP-9 gun gondola. All were shipped or flown in from the Soviet Union from early 1970 onwards, and installed at IAF Base Repair Depots, along with the associated radar-ranging predictor sight. The time-table for manufacture of the K-13A missile at Balanagar has not been disclosed, but the author was assured that HAL-built missiles were in use by December 1971. A reluctance to go into detail on the subject of K-13A reliability might be construed as

LEFT
*A Tatra fuel bowser tops up a MiG-21 PFM (SPS) of the Czech CL. The engine afterburner primary nozzle can be seen inside the revised circular rear end of the fuselage*

**LEFT**
*Another view of No 7910.
a PFM (SPS) of the CL
(Czech air force). Auxiliary
inlet covers are tied together
with a warning flag; even
the nose boom has a tailored
cover
(Robert J Ruffle archives)*

**RIGHT**
*An earlier PF of the Czech
CL, with the unblown
track-mounted slotted flaps.
Gears are retracting*

**BELOW**
*Winching the KM-1 seat
out of a Polish RF. These
MiG-21s have wingtip
RWR pods
(Robert J Ruffle archives)*

TOP
*Another Polish seat-winching operation, in this case with the original SK-1 seat, which is coming out of a MiG-21F with the final broad fin*
*(Robert J Ruffle archives)*

ABOVE
*A PFM (SPS) of the Polish PWL, in its usual configuration with centreline tank but no missiles*
*(Robert J Ruffle archives)*

RIGHT
*With tanks and anti-tank guns in the background, this MiG-21PFS forms part of a row of MiG fighters at the Soviet Museum of the Armed Forces*

OVERLEAF
*These PWL (Polish AF) groundcrew appear to have been manhandling this PF into position. It is an early model, with intermediate fin and original braking-parachute installation. Note how rudders are all hard-over to starboard*
*(Wozskowa Agensia via William Green)*

indicating that this factor was unimpressive in the 1970s, but if that is the case—and such a conclusion is in any case speculation—one must remember the abysmal performance of both the early versions of AIM-9 Sidewinder and also the extremely costly AIM-7 Sparrow in US service in Vietnam. Certainly, there has been no reluctance to talk about the gun pod, which is described as outstanding in all respects. It is loosely said to have 'the firepower of three Adens for the weight of one', and the IAF was particularly gratified at the small effect it had on the FL's performance. Good pilots soon found they could make near-perfect scores even at large deflection angles, the effective range extending to 1300 m (4,265 ft).

There is no doubt that this gondola mentally doubled the armament in the minds of the pilots, and in practice may have done even more than this. Introduction to service was very smooth indeed, IAF squadrons Nos 1, 4, 8, 29, 30, 45 and 47 all converting to the nimble supersonic fighter from such types as the Vampire, Toofani (Ouragan) and Mystere IVA in the course of 1968–72, as well as completing the equipment of No 28 which served as the trials and pilot conversion unit to back up the extremely stilted conversion courses in the Soviet Union at Tashkent and Lugovaya. Of course, the IAF pilots and many ground personnel had to learn the Cyrillic alphabet and quite a lot of Russian in the early days, though one of the tasks successfully accomplished at HAL and the IAF was to switch to English for all instruments, labels, stencils and instructions.

In the late 1960s pilot conversion in India began with prolonged classroom work to learn the Soviet alphabet and all necessary technical features of the aircraft, including a 'plain man's guide' to its aerodynamics and handling. Next came 10 hours in the standard imported simulator, followed by from two to four trips in a MiG-21U (these versions are described later) devoted mainly to aerobatics and instrument flight. The conversion is completed by not less than 10 hours on the FL itself, on completion of which the pilot would join a combat squadron. There seems to be no record of any pilot experiencing difficulty in converting from older and much slower aircraft.

HAL tried, generally successfully, to maintain a high standard of exterior finish in their FLs, which were delivered unpainted except for insignia and stencils. Even the dielectric fin cap was greyish glassfibre, so the only areas of contrasting colour were the inlet lip and glassfibre radome. Everyone, especially on the squadrons, was intensely proud of the new MiGs, and the various shortcomings were seldom discussed. These shortcomings were real enough. One was that, despite the massive and conservative design of almost everything, the maintenance burden was still high, many items being inspected every 50 hours and a full engine overhaul being required every 250 hours. The armament

situation was still not really satisfactory. With the GP-9 pack and two K-13s the feeling of relative nakedness was overcome, but nobody could pretend that the Type 77 was a true all-weather interceptor. This was before the importance of 'look down, shoot down' capability was widely appreciated, otherwise the MiG's shortcomings would have been even more apparent. The basic difficulties were the rather primitive form of radar, which demanded intense concentration by the pilot on a display that needed skill and practice to interpret accurately; the basically limited useful load, which made training sorties with the full kit of two missiles, the gun gondola and two tanks an extremely rare event; the very limited flight endurance, especially in the hot sky at low to medium altitudes; and also the widespread rumours emanating from the West to the effect that the Sidewinder AAM seldom performed properly, and this inevitably cast doubts in the minds of the IAF whose missiles were, with rare exceptions, to be carried but not to be fired.

The point must also be made that the IAF pilots expected to pick up a tremendous amount of the very latest 'gen' on air combat tactics from their Soviet instructors. Times have changed today, and with the MiG-27M and MiG-29 it is a very different story, but in the early years of MiG-21 training the input from the Soviet tutors was an intense disappointment. There were several reasons for this. Until the early 1970s it had been universal policy for all Soviet military personnel, not excluding NCOs and junior officers, to be instructed rather in the way small children learn multiplication tables. It would not be uncommon for classrooms of men destined for the most technically complex duties to spend weeks chanting the correct answers in unison. The wording had to be exact: one suspects that no attempt was made to explain underlying principles but merely to remember what was chanted. When this philosophy is extended to how to fly a supersonic fighter the result tends to be an approach of extreme conservatism. Doing everything 'by the book' was vital; any deep thought about how to get the best out of one's aircraft, or even 'hack' an unusual situation, was simply not part of the syllabus.

This goes down well with Soviet recruits, and caused no problems with pupils from non-technical

TOP
*These PWL (Polish air force) PFs are of an early standard, with intermediate fin (with a retroactively fitted fin-cap aerial and VHF mast amidships), and the original flaps and braking parachute (Robert J Ruffle archives)*

RIGHT
*In contrast, these PWL MiGs are typical of the ultimate member of the Ye-7 family, the PFM (SPS). Polish industry fought to build the '21' under licence but failed even to get contracts for spare parts*

*Soviet Frontal Aviation uses several kinds of hardened aircraft shelter, but this semicircular pattern in reinforced concrete (the outside deeply covered in earth) appears to be the most common. This early PF's pilot wears an anti-G suit. Note the 'standard of excellence' badge on the nose (Tass)*

*Aircraft 702, 703 and 726 of the Yugoslav air force are among the very latest Ye-7 aircraft (PFM-SPS), seen here landing with flap blowing (which comes on at this 30° setting) but no airbrake. Note the GP-9 gun pods (via Robert J Ruffle)*

Third World countries converting to earlier MiG fighters, but it was like a douche of cold water to the Indians. These men were not raw recruits but seasoned fighter pilots. They had to a man learned their trade in the way taught in the RAF, where a grasp of the fundamentals is regarded as being as important as the encouragement of individual initiative and decision-taking (without for a moment countenancing breaches of inflight discipline). The author can recall the incredulity with which his unruly squadron, forced into a classroom, were actually given the command 'pencils down' by a wingless education officer. This typifies what happened to the Indians at Lugovaya and Tashkent. Never for a moment was there any open resistance, but all the early courses of IAF pilots had to plead to try to learn something useful.

One must remember that these pilots fully expected war with Pakistan or East Pakistan to break out at any time. It was a matter of life and death that they should be able to fly their new MiG to the limits and know just what it could, or could not, do. This their Soviet instructors never for a moment considered. The basic conversion course—which, whilst following a rigid set of rules also often seemed rather uncertain, because not all instructors were agreed on precisely what these rules were—was conservative to an extreme degree. This was not because of the high value placed on MiG-21s or on individual human lives, but because of the deep-seated Russian way in which instruction was done. The course was not designed for experienced, aggressive, free-thinking fighter jocks!

Early in the first course quite senior IAF officers caused consternation among the school staff by daring to try to discover how high a MiG-21F could climb, and how fast it would go. This consternation was not at all because the answers were very disappointing. In clean condition the fuel state quickly became critical, and long before reaching the brochure limits of 60,000 ft (18,300 m) and Mach 2.2. Admittedly it did seem possible to get the Mach needle to 1.9, but nobody managed to get the altimeter reading above 46,000 ft (14,000 m). The trouble was caused by the fact that exploring any kind of limits was absolutely *verboten*! Indeed, at least until

the mid-1970s trainee MiG-21 pilots were forbidden to loop or to roll at a rate exceeding 90°/sec, and especially prohibited from entering cloud or even flying on the quite adequate blind-flying panel.

The IAF pupils had to beg to be allowed to indulge in simulated air combat. In 1975 the magazine *Flight International* reported an IAF pilot as saying 'The Russians seemed to teach only a single fast attacking pass, followed by a rather uncertain—and suicidally indecisive—breakaway. Although the training area was only five minutes' flying away from the Russian base, special arrangements were made to hold these practice dogfights over the field in order to conserve fuel'. The author discussed this later with the Soviet Air Attache in London who frankly admitted the perhaps overcautious approach to training all students, and especially foreign ones. He said 'I think we would rather that foreign pilots should work out their own air combat methods'. This is certainly what happened in the case of the IAF, which decided to form TACDE (Tactics and Combat Development Establishment) in order to work out the best procedures for its own combat aircraft, especially the MiG-21 and Su-7B.

One thing the Indian pilots were, reluctantly, permitted to do by Soviet instructors was to drop bombs and fire rockets, though normally only to the extent of four practice bombs and one (sometimes two) salvoes from a UV-16-57 launcher. No K-13A missiles were even carried during training sorties, far less fired, so IAF pilots could not even practise listening to the various growls and singing noises in the headset indicating the degrees of lock-on of the missile's seeker head. Missile training was an important part of the curriculum during weapon training with the IAF MiG-21 squadrons, though actual firing of these weapons—expensive in comparison with other IAF stores, though in fact by far the cheapest AAMs ever deployed—was very strictly rationed. Even the 23 mm ammunition had to be fired in extremely short bursts, though these were

LEFT
*These LSK (East German AF) pilots wear plain overalls and bonedome, unlike the near-astronaut garb of the Frontal Aviation pilot on page 90. The early PF has no S-3M RWR installation*

UPPER RIGHT
*In contrast. LSK No 758 is a late model PFM (SPS), seen here landing without external load. SPS reduces the landing AOA by about 5, giving a better view*

RIGHT
*C1135 of the Indian AF is a very late Model 77, here showing off its cruciform braking parachute. K-13As are are on board*

sufficient to confirm that the GP-9 could be aimed accurately and hardly ever interfered with engine behaviour.

As noted previously, Soviet flight simulators were used to assist pilot conversion, and the IAF workshops even created training simulators of Indian design to assist with some aspects of weapons and systems. No MiG-21 OCU was set up; instead, pilots complete their original training courses on two-seat and single-seat Hunters to become qualified as 'Fully

Ops, Day' pilots. Those selected for the MiG then go to their squadron and convert via simulators and the two-seat MiG Type 66-400 or 66-600 (MiG-21U), before getting to grips with the single-seater. At first there was plenty to learn. Not only did the newly posted MiG-21 pilot have to become proficient with the radar and AAMs but he also, before 1968, had to conduct seemingly endless attack sorties dropping practice bombs and firing 57 mm rockets, the latter often being loaded only two or three in each launcher.

After 1968 the massive Su-7BM 'Whale' arrived to take over the attack mission, which undoubtedly helped the MiG squadrons to hone their air combat skills more effectively.

The expected war with Pakistan finally erupted on 3 December 1971. By this time the MiG force was formidable, with eight squadrons operationally ready on the FL Type 76: Nos 1, 4, 8, 28, 29, 30, 45 and 47. Five of these were deployed along the western front, on air defence, while the other three were facing East

*Pilots of Red Dragon squadron of the Indian Air Force are briefed before a mission in the brief war with Pakistan. All these Type 77s (including C588, 776 and 736) were assembled by HAL from Soviet-supplied components. IFF is Western*

Pakistan and tasked with ground attack as well as air combat. On the western front, some 700 miles in length, the MiG-21s were busy from Day 1. In an endeavour to entice PAF fighters into battle numerous deep penetrations were made at heights from 7 to 10 km (23,000–33,000 ft), there being no SAM threat to worry about. Pairs of MiGs escorted small attack forces of Su-7s, Hunters and Maruts, while others acted as high-altitude VHF relay stations with a direct line-of-sight link to IAF attacking aircraft penetrating Pakistan at low level, below the horizon to the controlling stations in the Punjab. These MiGs were known as Sparrows, and were denounced by Pakistan as Soviet-flown Tu-126 'Moss' AWACS aircraft, a report picked up by world news services and giving rise to the popular belief that such aircraft really did fly on the Indian side in 1971.

Prior to the start of hostilities almost every MiG-21 and Su-7 in IAF front-line squadrons had been rather roughly sprayed with green/brown camouflage, though the Hunters and Canberras remained in their glossy green/grey applied in the British factories, and the Maruts, Gnats and MiG-21U Type 66 trainers all remained natural metal. The hasty painting was done on the squadron flight-lines, and was far from uniform. Not only the patterns but the colours varied quite widely, and some of the busiest MiGs never got painted at all, especially the ones on the eastern front.

Dozens of books and magazine articles have been written about this brief war, and it is sad that to this day there are such high feelings about who did what, and where truth lies, that correspondents who covered the war from one side are *persona non grata* with the other. Certainly the contemporary accounts from the IAF side make no mention of any MiGs being shot down, and even those written with the benefit of hindsight—such as that by Pushpindar Chopra published by *Air Enthusiast* for July 1973— make no reference to any MiG losses, or to any air combat where the MiG came off second-best.

Certainly there was no lack of enthusiasm on the part of the MiG drivers. They knew they had a pretty good fighter, well shaken down in service, now with adequate armament and—so far as they could see— no real shortcomings. They were convinced it could outfly the PAF Mirage IIIs, and expected to 'fly rings round' the few F-104As. Other opposition, such as the F-6 (Chinese-built MiG-19SF) and F-86F, was hardly taken seriously. Everyone was desperate to prove what the new MiG-21 could do, but for a while not much happened. In the Eastern Air Command the MiGs were heavily engaged in attack on surface targets, meeting very little opposition, but in the West there were large concentrations of PAF airpower. Many MiG sorties on this enormous front (see map) were deep penetrations with the express purpose of drawing the PAF into battle. According to the IAF, the enemy was very reluctant to do this, an impression utterly at variance with that gained by one

of Britain's most respected aviation writers, John Fricker, when he wrote a detailed on-the-spot account of the 1971 air war.

To cite one instance, on 7 December 1971 Pakistani ground forces claimed a MiG-21 over Chamb, said to have been 'admitted' by India. Yet in the article mentioned above written 18 months later by Chopra this MiG is reported as having been 'nursed back to its base, where it was found to have sustained three large gashes . . .' Another example that shows the problems faced by the researcher concerns the first victim to fall before a MiG-21. In

C529, a Type 77 of the Indian Air Force, gives a perfect illustration of how the landing gears tuck away as the system is cycled during major maintenance. The seat has been removed and bracing struts clamped on the nosecone. In the rear is a Type 66 trainer

his 1973 story Chopra describes how (apparently on the afternoon of 6 December, though this is not explicitly stated) IAF Flt Lt S B Shah escorting HF-24s near Mirpur Khas, found three F-6s closing from astern. Eventually Shah was able to get in 'a burst of 23 mm from about 600 m'. The F-6 rolled over and went straight in. Yet in Chopra's day-by-day account of the air war written just a year earlier (*Air Enthusiast*, April 1972) there is no mention of such a combat.

Yet another oddity is that in the 1972 war diary Chopra reported that on 12 December 'Air combat took place near the port of Sikka, 40 miles from the Jamnagar airfield, between MiG-21s and Star-fighters, one of the Starfighters being shot down and its pilot captured.' Yet in his 1973 account Chopra gives a different conclusion, which has also been reported by others. This brief encounter, at zero feet over the Gulf of Kutch, was the meeting between the MiG-21FL and the F-104A that aviation buffs around the world had been waiting for. Incidentally the F-104s on this southern part of the main front were a batch of ten which King Hussein of Jordan lent to Pakistan at the start of the war.

According to IAF reports, at about 14:00 local time on 12 December, observation posts on the north side of the Gulf reported two F-104s flying south, very low and fast, obviously bent on attacking airfields or ports on the south side. Flt Lts Saigal and Soni were scrambled from Jamnagar, climbed to 6,000 ft (1830 m) over the airfield and were about to start a CAP orbit when the first 104 was seen streaking in for a strafing run. Soni dived after it in full afterburner, switching missiles and gun to FIRE. Saigal radioed that the second 104 had abandoned its attack run and was making off to the north at about Mach 1. Soni's quarry turned through almost a complete circle but the MiG had no difficulty staying with the Lockheed and rolled out behind it on a northerly heading at extremely low level, still in full afterburner and at close to Mach 1. Surprisingly, with such a perfect infrared target, Soni selected GUNS. At about 900 m range—at which an F-104 in afterburner seen from astern looks like a mere tiny orange spot—Soni fired a long burst. Soni must have had remarkable luck at this range, because the 104 flamed almost at once, and went straight in. At the last moment the pilot ejected, but it cannot have done him much good, because the F-104A seat ejects downward, and the Gulf of Kutch is notorious for sharks.

Of course, Soni's colleagues were jubilant, but this had not really been a combat in the accepted sense, merely the rather lucky destruction at extreme range of an enemy running for his life. It had, however, suggested that at high IAS the MiG could easily turn inside the small-winged Lockheed, though this was no more than might have been expected. Certainly the most remarkable feature of the encounter was getting strikes almost from the first round on such a tiny and elusive target. It seems impossible today to

get confirmation of the fact, but common sense suggests that ejection downwards at about Mach 0.95 from just above the wavetops into shark-infested water is not likely lead to survival as a POW!

The only other MiG versus F-104 combats came on the very last day of the war, 17 December 1971. Sqn Ldr I S Bindra, CO of No 29 'Black Scorpion' squadron, operating from Uttarslai, had just taken off on a CAP in support of a Marut strike when he was advised of the high-Mach approach of a lone F-104 (which in fact made no attack on the airfield). Bindra went into afterburner and descended to go after the speeding 104. He fired a K-13A but the missile failed to achieve lock. His second missile did lock-on, and exploded near the F-104's cockpit. As the Starfighter continued to fly, though 'unsteadily', Bindar tried a burst of gunfire at a high angle-off. By this time the F-104 was pouring smoke, and it crashed into sandhills a few miles further on.

Later on the same day two other 29 Sqn pilots, Flt Lts N Kukreja and A Datta, were escorting Maruts and approaching Umarkot when they met two F-104s head-on. One of the bogeys appeared to launch an ineffectual AAM (it could only have been a Sidewinder, almost identical to the K-13A), and very soon all four aircraft were roughly in a stern chase in the sequence: No 2 F-104, Kukreja's MiG, No 1 F-104 (the AAM firer), and Datta's MiG. Datta found himself overtaking fast, at a height of some 1,600 ft, and at the same moment realized he was in K-13A firing parameters, as indicated by both the radar display and his headset audio note. He fired both. He was just switching his firing selector over to the gun when the F-104 vanished in a fireball. Meanwhile Kukreja had likewise found himself rapidly overhauling his own F-104, but suddenly felt a judder run through his MiG. Afterwards it was thought this may have been reaction of the nosecone to sudden disturbed air caused by a burst of gunfire from the F-104 behind him (downed seconds later by Datta). Instruments seemed normal, so Kukreja fired a missile, followed about five seconds later by another. The first failed, but the second held its lock and exploded very close to the F-104, which spiralled down into the ground. The whole action had taken much less than two minutes.

A ceasefire came into effect at 20:00 hr on the same day, and subsequently both sides published wildly differing figures for air victories and losses. Those published by Pakistan appeared to be far better documented, but inspection of the serial numbers of some downed MiGs (C-116 and C-7641) suggests that these do not fit in with any MiG numbers seen elsewhere. According to the Pakistanis nine MiG-21FLs were shot down on the Western front alone, and two of these were claimed by aircraft of the PAF. On 14 December an F-6 flown by Flt Lt Aamer claimed one, using a Sidewinder, and on the last day Flt Lt Maqsood Amir's F-86F destroyed a MiG over Pasrur, the pilot being captured. The interesting

thing is that both sides expressed themselves very well pleased with their equipment. The PAF frankly admitted the poor manoeuvrability of the F-104A, but equally pointed out the far superior manoeuvrability in a dogfight of the F-6 and F-86. Again this is not news to any student of aircraft design. If almost any Mach-2 fighter were to 'mix it' with an F-6 or F-86 it would inevitably be out-turned, though modern fighters such as the F-16 have such excess power that they could probably get out of trouble, especially by using the vertical plane.

According to the PAF it was offered the MiG-21 in 1968 but rejected it. Deficiencies were then held to include: ineffective radar below about 3,000 ft (750 m) because of ground clutter, and a maximum lock-on range of less than eight miles (this is called 'nonsense' by the Russians); poor pilot view both ahead and to the rear (which is indisputable); high fuel consumption, especially at low level (to which the IAF retorts that 'in every combat with the F-104 or F-6 it was the PAF fighter that sought to disengage first'); lack of internal gun armament, and ammunition for only about four seconds in those MiGs

*There has seldom been much detailed information on the operations of the air force of the People's Army of North Vietnam. That air force appeared to prefer the MiG-17, but here are two of its early PFs, with SK-1 seat and K-13A missiles fitted*

fitted with the GP-9 gondola; and low level speed limit of only 593 knots (to which the IAF can fairly reply that the MiG had no difficulty at all in catching everything with a green and white roundel).

One ought not to draw too many conclusions from so few and such brief encounters. In most cases, where the PAF aircraft tried to use its Mach 2 speed it got shot down. In contrast, the older F-6 and F-86 scored 2-nil. There was no encounter between a MiG and a Mirage.

Thus, the Indo-Pakistan war of December 1971 is a matter for speculation and argument, but it is much better documented than most of the other MiG-21 conflicts! In Vietnam the People's Army Air Force has predictably shown itself good at putting out poor photographs with vague but heroic captions, but very short on fact. Almost the only kind of historical record seems to be an article by Gen-Maj Dao Din Luen, C-in-C of the VPAAF, published rather unexpectedly in a 1980 edition of the Soviet *Aviatsiya i Kosmonavtika*. Even this is incredibly vague, and while places and pilots tend to be mentioned, dates and aircraft types are not! Certainly the MiG-17 was used in much larger numbers than the MiG-21, so it would be rash to ascribe any particular engagement to one of the latter. A second factor is the almost total inexperience of the VPAAF pilots, which largely negated any advantages possessed by their aircraft.

Starting with a kill by an F-4C on 26 April 1966, the US Air Force, Navy and Marine Corps fighter pilots in Vietnam were credited with 68 MiG-21s, the majority being PFs though in combat reports nobody went beyond the portmanteau word 'Fishbed'. The one period when the MiG-21 proved to have a sting was, according to US records, the seven months starting August 1967, when VPAAF MiG-21s working in pairs at very low level devised a method of making a single supersonic firing pass through formations of anything from A-1s to F-105s, scoring (even by American reckoning) 18 kills for only five losses. The curious thing is that most of the successful engagements during this period, according to Gen Luen (who surely ought to know) happened in the *spring* of 1967, such as the destruction of four F-105s on 30 April and three F-4s on 12 May.

Right at the end of the US involvement, MiG-21s were used to shadow B-52s on their heavy night raids and, it was said by the Americans, radio back the proper detonating altitude for the SAMs. This seems nonsense, because the V750Vk SAM system is perfectly capable of working out target heights for itself. What is more interesting is that, while a B-52D tail gunner, on the evening of the first day (18 December 1972) claimed and was credited with the destruction of a MiG-21 which was never recorded as missing by the VPAAF, the VPAAF for its part credited Hero of the People's Army Fam Tuan with the destruction of a B-52 which was never admitted by the USAF! Assuming that Fam Tuan's claim was justified, and there is no reason to doubt it, then one B-52 credited to SAMs actually fell to an enemy night fighter.

For the record, the two top-scoring VPAAF pilots, Col Tomb (13-plus, and eventually shot down by US ace Randy Cunningham USN) and Capt Nguyen Van Bay, were exclusively exponents of the MiG-17.

In the Arab/Israeli 'Six-Day War' of 5–10 June 1967 the dominant event was the massive and sustained pre-emptive strike by the Israeli *Chel Ha'Avir* against all the surrounding UAR (United Arab Republic) air forces. In the space of some three hours over 300 UAR aircraft were destroyed, for the loss of 19 Israeli machines. Few Egyptian or Syrian fighters managed to get into the air. The very first casualty of the war was thought to have been a MiG-21 of Egypt's 45 Sqn caught as it took off from Abu Sueir, and another was destroyed there minutes later as it tried to land on the cratered runway. At Inchas three MiG-21FLs of 40 Sqn managed to get airborne between the craters immediately after the first wave of attacks, one shooting down an Ouragan over Cairo West. After the second wave, at 10:01 hrs, another managed to get airborne from the completely wrecked airbase and shot down a Mystere just outside the perimeter; but minutes later the last two serviceable MiG-21s were blasted by a Mirage IIICJ just as they reached the shattered runway. How bad things were is graphically portrayed by the photograph of four burned-out MiG-21s on just one small bit of Abu Sueir apron. In fact the Israeli destruction at this airfield was not yet over, because at 10:30 a large group of MiG-21s and the MiG-19SFs of No 20 Sqn, which had urgently flown up from Hurghada in the south, were bounced by Mirages as they tried to land. Four were shot down at once, and the rest were put out of action in trying to land on the blasted runways or in belly landings on running out of fuel.

On the far north-east front the Syrians were in the process of converting their critically small number of fighter pilots—barely half the number needed to operate their two full-strength fighter squadrons—from the MiG-21F to the PF. As the Israelis could not hit everywhere at once the Syrians escaped on the morning of 5 June, and at 11:45 a dozen MiG-21PFs bombed the oil refinery at Haifa and strafed Mahanayim airbase, but retribution was not long in coming. By 13:00 all Syrian airfields except distant T4 had been hit, and T4 was attended to in mid-afternoon. Though damage was far from total, the Syrians lost two-thirds of their front-line strength on that first day.

For the rest of that brief war the combined and once mighty airpower of the UAR managed no more than the occasional pinprick. Almost the last MiG-21s to get into the air were two Egyptian PFs which at 05:36 on Day 2 tried to strafe the incoming Israeli army near Bir Lahfan. Both were caught by Mirages. Another (possibly the last airworthy) PF was shot down on 7 June as it escorted an Il-28 trying to bomb the occupied airfield of El Arish.

This war remains, probably for all time, as the classic example of the pre-emptive strike. The UAR, essentially Egypt and Syria, put its house in order, had its losses made good by the Soviet Union, and not only got down to hard training but painted a new unified UAR insignia to show the degree of integrated control that had been achieved. UAR forces were built up massively, with many new weapons such as Tu-16s with 'Kelt' stand-off missiles, SA-6 and Hawk SAMs with deadly continuous-wave guidance, and hordes of ZSU-23-4 mobile flak vehicles and Frog anti-airfield rockets. At last all was ready, and the great plan agreed. All hell was let loose at 14:05 on 6 October 1973. It was *Yom Kippur*, the special holy day in the Jewish calendar, and to say Israel was caught off-balance is an understatement. Over 100 MiG-21s were among the

222 Egyptian aircraft that mounted the opening assault, which took in three of the chief *Chel Ha'Avir* airbases (Bir Thamada, El Mulayz and El Sur). But though the UAR forces had things almost entirely their own way on the opening day, things got much harder on 7 October and from that day on the MiG-21s were almost exclusively reserved for top cover, leaving the dangerous attack missions to the MiG-17s, Su-7BMs and Hunters.

By 10 October there was no more fast movement. The war had degenerated into a slogging match, in which the brilliantly professional *Chel Ha'Avir*—nothing like knocked out by the pre-emptive strike—largely redressed the balance. Lebanese observers reported that a large air battle near their frontier with Syria on 10 October, mainly involving Mirages and MiG-21s, ended in a clear-cut Syrian victory, but such a report must be viewed with suspicion. On the other hand a single Egyptian squadron at Mansurah claimed 59 kills, and another at Inchas had film to support its claim of 22 confirmed, both being MiG-21 units. At ceasefire on 24 October the final tally of losses was said by Western observers to have been: Egypt, 223 plus 42 helicopters, Syria 118 plus 13, Iraq 21, Libya and Algeria (who sent expeditionary forces) 30, and Israel 106 plus six helicopters. Whereas nearly all the UAR losses were due to the Israeli fighter pilots, nearly all the *Chel Ha'Avir* losses were due to SAMs and flak. But this does not reflect badly on the MiG-21, and a fair assessment by a senior Israeli Mirage pilot is that the MiG-21 could manoeuvre 'at least as well' as the best Mirage, but that Israel definitely had the edge in AAMs and, to an even greater degree, in pilots.

Early MiG-21s have been involved in many other conflicts, some of them large-scale wars. One example is Angola where, after the departure of the Portuguese colonial power in November 1975, the Marxist MPLA, massively backed by Cuba and the Soviet Union, initially had things almost entirely its own way, and a force which certainly exceeded 40 MiG-21Fs and PFs and according to some reports numbered as many as 70, were hardly needed. Subsequently the opposition parties, FNLA and UNITA, took over control of more than half the strife-torn country, and while the number of MiG-21s has probably fallen to about 30 these are now mainly of later variants, and they have been in sporadic action against both the opposition armies and against South African forces in Namibia.

Another strife-torn area is the Horn of Africa, where simmering border conflicts between Ethiopia

*Another picture from North Vietnam. It is surely strange that, while 4128 and 4227 carry combat-ready K-13A missiles, and the ground crew wear steel helmets, the aircraft are parked together in the open with no camouflage or shelter?*

and Somalia, mainly over historic claims to land in the Ogaden, erupted into a full-scale air war on 24 July 1977. To say the situation was involved is to put it mildly, for there had been coups and civil wars in both countries. Despite this the Soviet Union jumped in eagerly and supplied both sides with masses of war material, the aircraft including a total of over 100 MiG-21s. Little reliable detail has emerged from the resulting nine years of bitter fighting, though on 27 July 1977 there was certainly a dogfight between Somali MiG-21s and Ethiopian F-5As. By the end of the first week Ethiopia admitted losing three of the six F-5s claimed by Somalia, and in reply claimed eight MiG-21s. At the end of three months Ethiopia's fragile air force had been bolstered

*No explanation can be obtained of how this missile-toting MiG-21PF was photographed by the US Air Force near Hanoi on 4 January 1967. The aspect appears to be from directly overhead*
*(USAF via Robert F Dorr)*

by not only MiG-21s but also MiG-23s flown by Cuban mercenaries, and Somali MiG losses were said to range upwards from 20.

Yet another MiG-versus-MiG situation erupted just three days earlier, on 21 July 1977, when tension between Egypt and Libya reached breaking point. In the air sporadic battles took place, Libyan SA-7s claiming a MiG-21 while Egypt claimed a MiG-23 and Mirage. On the following day Libya claimed eight, including three MiG-21s, in Egyptian attacks on coastal targets; Egypt said the raids were 'a figment of the imagination'. Fighting went on until the 24th, by which time Libyan claims reached 25, including seven MiG-21s (Egypt merely admitted losing two Su-20s). It all supported the belief that large numbers of MiGs ranged along disputed frontiers are bad news for peace. Incidentally, the first claim of one MiG-21 downing another was reported by Pakistan. According to the PAF, when two MiG-21s were scrambled at night to intercept a Mirage IIIEP, one of them downed his No 2 with an AAM!

# Chapter 7
# The Ye-8 family

This is a fairly brief chapter because none of the members of this interesting group entered production. Few details are available about them, but they might have diverted the MiG-21 development along entirely different paths.

The Ye-8 itself was a Ye-7 development aircraft used as the basis for two proposed families of future production versions dating from about 1960. One, the MiG-21I, remains a mystery. The common meaning of I is *istrebitel* (fighter), which is what the MiG-21 was already. Of the other we do have a few clues. Designated MiG-21Sht (*shturmovik*, armoured assaulter), it was to be a close-support machine to operate from front-line airstrips against surface targets. Indeed East German reports have translated Sht as 'schlacht', meaning close-support, though the Soviets do not use the German language to designate their warplanes. The original notion of heavy armour had by 1960 given way to mere enhanced protection of vital areas, because the MiG-21 had very little weapon payload capability even without the burden of armour.

During World War 2 the most famous *shturmovik*, the Il-2, had sustained a record production run of 36,163 aircraft, having been described by Stalin as 'needed by the Red Army like it needs air and bread'. By the time the MiG-15 came along, shortly after the war, it was gradually realized that the new breed of simple jet fighters could do excellent work in the close-support mission, and all specialized *shturmoviks* (notably the Il-40) were cancelled. The MiG-21Sht seemed a natural development, with still further improved short-field capability, varied attack weapon loads, high-flotation landing gears for operation from soft surfaces and enhanced local protection. The Ye-7 was modified as the Ye-8 and flown in 1962 to test some of the attack version's new features.

The obvious new feature was that it was fitted with canards, following research at the OKB and at TsAGI. These were fully powered and used as primary pitch control surfaces, and they also increased lift on takeoff by lifting the front of the aircraft instead of pushing down at the back, as did the original tailplanes. The latter were retained, but no longer had anti-flutter masses at the tips. Whether the tailplanes were locked at neutral incidence is not publicly known, but that might explain absence of tip masses. On the other hand, there is no objection to using foreplanes and tailplanes simultaneously; indeed the author has long believed there is a case for aircraft that possess both a foreplane and a tailplane. Certainly, if one had to remove one of those auxiliary surfaces it should be the tailplane, which is a most undesirable attribute which actually pushes downwards at the very times an aircraft most needs all the lift it can get, on takeoff and landing. The Ye-8 has been verbally described to the author as having STOL performance, and one would expect it to be better in this regard than regular MiG-21s.

Compared with today's breed of canard fighters the foreplanes of the Ye-8 were far from the wing, right in the nose where their effective moment arm was very large (almost exactly the same as that of the tailplanes). They were cropped deltas mounted in the mid-position, and driven by the same duplex hydraulics as the other flight control surfaces. At semi-span (measured from the root) each surface carried a long forward-facing rod looking exactly like an anti-flutter mass. This is probably what they were, and they would also have had the effect of mass-balancing the surface about its rotation spigot, but to mount such masses so far forward and so far inboard on short-span rigid canards is surprising to say the least.

Of course the canards would not only greatly assist takeoff and landing, both in reducing ground run and fuselage nose-up attitude, but they would also

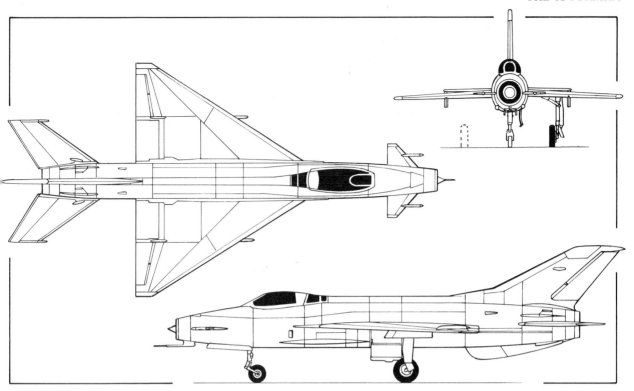

TOP

*A three-view of the prototype Ye-8: design objectives were shorter field length with (if possible) increased external weapon loads*

ABOVE

*So far as the author knows neither of the drawings on this page has ever appeared previously (and an even less-familiar one appears overleaf). The subject in this case is the MiG-21DPD, or Type 92 (a puzzling designation). It is shown in the jet-lift mode. Landing gears were fixed*

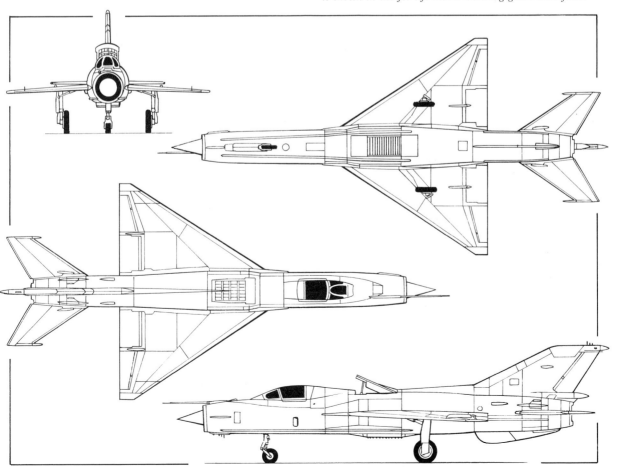

enhance combat manoeuvrability, especially with relatively heavy attack weapon loads. Mounted at the same level as the wing, they would, when powerfully deflected, also have sent back strong spiral vortices which would enhance flow over the wing roots, especially in extreme manoeuvres. It is again surprising that the idea was not pursued, because if competently executed it must surely have resulted in a superior aircraft.

There is little point in speculating on the Ye-8's other features. The viewpoint chosen for the only released photograph might be thought to suggest that it had an unconventional landing gear, though ramp launch can certainly be excluded as a possibility. The underwing stores are not K-13As but either superimposed attack rockets (*krupnokaliber* ones of 180 mm or 240 mm size) or very long pylons for carrying stores in tandem. The canards required relocation of the forward auxiliary inlet doors.

Later, around 1969, the MiG OKB built at least one further prototype to a more advanced design intended to offer enhanced performance in both fighter and ground-attack roles, and with the capability of carrying the large High Lark radar fire control as fitted to the MiG-23MF series. Believed to be the Ye-32, this aircraft combined the wings, main landing gear, rear fuselage and tail of the Ye-9 series MiG-21 with the foreplanes of the Ye-8 and a variable-geometry chin inlet leaving the nose completely free for the radar. The inlet duct bifurcated immediately to accommodate a central box for the relocated aft-retracting MiG-21 nose gear. Very little is known of this aircraft, thought to have been a one-off, though it is believed to have had the same arrangement of three airbrakes as the MiG-21. From the only known photograph it appears doubtful that there could have been an internal gun. The Ye-32 was probably the first canard supersonic fighter to fly in the Soviet Union, and the first in the world to have a powered control surface at nose and tail. Almost certainly it assisted the design of Sukhoi's Type 101 bomber and the parametric studies which led to the non-canard MiG-29.

Aviation policymakers have often acted in what seem strange ways. Aircraft have been built to try out some new idea. The results have exceeded all expectations. Reports are written, everyone says what a success it all was, and nothing more is done to put the idea to use. Possibly the Ye-8 fell into this category, and the MiG OKB has yet to proclaim a canard fighter. More probably, by 1962 the enormous influence of the TFX (F-111) was making the policymakers lose interest in anything that did not have a swing wing. The MiG OKB took this on board avidly.

BELOW
*Not a MiG-21 crossed with today's EAP but Mikoyan's Ye-32 configuration-research aircraft of more than 15 years ago. No high-quality photograph has yet appeared of this outwardly impressive machine, which was to have the capability of carrying a large multimode 'look down, shoot down' radar*

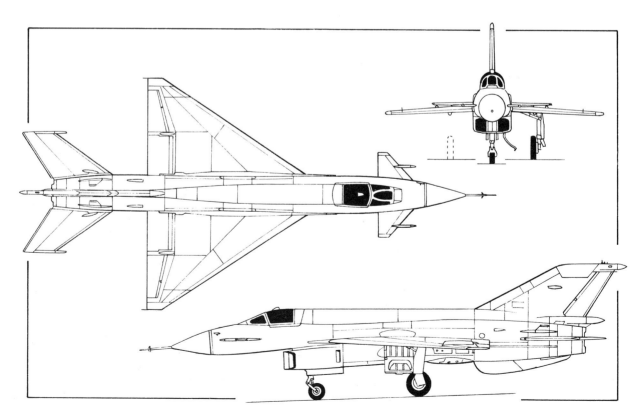

*A strange blend of MiG-21 and MiG-23, the Ye-230 incorporated the twin-jet lift bay amidships that is now, with modifications, used in the Yak-38 Forger. Major parts of this machine, called Faithless by NATO, were similar to MiG-21 parts but 25 per cent larger*

There was at this time another idea that was atracting enormous interest among all builders of combat aircraft. Jet lift appeared to open the way to airpower freed from the dangerous confines of fixed airbases and NATO was going mad with two BMRs (Basic Military Requirements) for a V/STOL fighter-bomber and a V/STOL transport. Inevitably Moscow followed suit, and most of the tactical OKBs—Mikoyan, Sukhoi and Yakovlev—built research aircraft to try out ideas. A N Rafaelyants had produced the original jet-lift Turbolyet back in 1957, which carried out the pioneer Soviet research into hovering jets with reaction controls. This provided a useful underpinning of knowledge for the jet-lift trials aircraft of the 1960s.

Mikoyan built at least two. One was a hybrid delta with a fuselage and tail related to the Ye-23/MiG-23 family. The other was the Type 92, or MiG-21DPD (*Dopelnitelnye Pod'yomnye Dvigatel*, supplementary lifting engines). This was a considerable rebuild of a MiG-21PFM. An extra bay 1.2 m long was spliced into the fuselage at the centre of gravity to house two lift engines, generally agreed to have been of 3500 kg thrust each and named in a Czech journal as type Koliesov ZM. Each was a simple turbojet, very like an enlarged RB.108 in design; indeed the entire lift-jet bay owed a great deal to that of the Shorts SC.1. The louvred dorsal door and exit nozzle box looked almost identical, though following an incident in which an SC.1 came heavily to earth because its inlets became clogged with fresh-cut grass the Soviet designers played safe and made their entire dorsal door open, hinging up from the rear throughout the lift-jet regime.

The start sequence was automatic, using ground electric power, though it was Mikoyan's wish to use air bleed from the main engine to spin the lift-jet turbines. The engines were installed sloping slightly backwards, and the tray under the fuselage was fitted with cascade vanes under pilot control for deflecting the lift jets to front or rear to provide acceleration or braking. In its one public display at Domodyedovo in 1967 famed test pilot Piotr Ostapyenko gave a restrained exposition and clearly had no intention of letting speed drop below about 100 km/h. SPS flaps were blown throughout, and prominent bleed pipes could be seen outside the fuselage leading to reaction control jets at nose and tail. No reaction valves could be seen near the wingtips, and so one can conclude that the 92 could not be flown slow enough for the ailerons to become ineffective, though any MiG-21 pilot will confirm that you begin to 'run out of aileron' at 240 km/h. Asymmetric flap blowing is surely a non-starter, so possibly the 92 was thought to manage without lateral control?

The rest of the aircraft was variously modified to suit the need. Adding a fuselage bay enabled most of the original tankage to be retained, but there was no room for mainwheels in the fuselage so the main legs were fixed. What was not explained was why they should have been moved outboard, increasing the track. The tyres were even larger than normal, as was the stroke of the soft oleos. An extra dorsal fin was added from the fin to the lift-jet door, and there was no provision for pylons. The author does not know the meaning of the badge painted each side of the nose and rear fuselage.

The author never spoke to Mikoyan about the DPD – it slipped his mind – and he would probably not have elicited helpful answers, but the historical record suggests increasing tendency on the part of the Soviet policymakers to take their cue from the West. American influence gradually killed NATO enthusiasm for jet-lift combat aircraft able to disperse away from airfields, and this almost certainly played a dominant part in snuffing out interest in the Soviet Union (except for shipboard operations). Certainly there was never the slightest suggestion that the DPD might have led direct to a production machine, but

the MiG OKB might have been expected to use the information gained in designing a completely new front-line machine with STOVL capability. The fact that nothing has appeared underscores the tremendous influence of US decisions on the Soviet Union, and probably has given rise to prolonged arguments behind the scenes. Very remarkably indeed, while continuing to pay lip service to the importance of off-airfield operation, and practising brief deployment from fields and highways, Frontal Aviation has no fixed-wing aircraft able to fly useful missions from even 1,640 ft (500 m) airstrips.

Another one-off research conversion, the A-144 or MiG-21 *Analog*, was a member of the Ye-9 family and so is discussed later.

RIGHT
*One of the most senior MiG OKB test pilots, Hero of the Soviet Union Piotr Ostapyenko gained many world records in such aircraft as the Ye-166, Ye-266 (MiG-25 related) and various MiG-21 prototypes. He handled much of the DPD test programme*
*(Tass)*

BELOW
*The author has no information on the badge painted on the nose and rear fuselage of the MiG-21DPD, here seen making a slow touchdown. This research machine was incapable of vertical or hovering flight*

# Chapter 8
# The Ye-9 family

The author only met Mikoyan once, in June 1969, and ever afterwards regretted what seemed a great missed opportunity. The famed Soviet designer was the antithesis of Antonov. Instead of enthusiastically wanting to communicate, he volunteered nothing, appered ill at ease and tended to reply with the fewest number of words possible (typically a yes or no). In the Soviet system, what you do not say cannot be used against you, yet several other heads of Soviet OKBs have demonstrated that it is still possible in these circumstances to give a good press conference.

One of the author's questions to Mikoyan was 'Have you not been surprised at the long life of the MiG-21 through successive generations?' At this Mikoyan appeared to struggle inwardly for several seconds; eventually he said 'Nyet'.

This seemed like one of the missed opportunities, because, in comparison with the roughly contemporary Western fighters, such as the F-104, F-4 and Mirage III, the MiG-21 has been developed over a longer period, through more distinct sub-families, and with greater advance in all-round capability. On the basis of one broad-brush parameter, engine thrust, the MiG-21 has always been very competitive. The only fighters with a strictly comparable growth in power and capability appear to have been the Spitfire and Bf 109, and their entire life histories encompassed a mere dozen years. The MiG-21 was developed for 30 years.

In the course of this long period the appearance and character of the MiG-21 changed tremendously, so that at any given point in time it still seemed to be competitive, and the kind of fighter that would not make its pilot feel a second-class citizen. There are very strict limits to how far this can be done. Sudden bold changes, such as stretching the fuselage and fitting two engines (see the final chapter) are often self-defeating and do little except add cost. What usually does achieve success is to study the detail

engineering and introduce small changes to rectify known deficiencies. This is what was done to the World War 2 fighters just mentioned, and the same philosophy was followed by the MiG OKB (indeed, it is the invariable method adopted by Soviet design teams).

Throughout the MiG-21 story the whole process of development was made more difficult by the fact that basic design was in many ways marginal. When you are so critical on weight that you take out one of your two guns you clearly do not have a lot of leeway to play with. From the very start it was clear the MiG-21 was never going to be in the class of the US fighters which almost casually can tote five tons or more of bombs or external fuel. Having accepted that what had been created was a bit of a lightweight—though perhaps not quite as useless as the Indian pilot's 'supersonic sports plane'—the MiG OKB then proceeded with typical Soviet methodical plodding to make it better and better.

Throughout, the splendid Tumanskii engine KB played a central role in coming up with a succession of engines which were improved across-the-board. These engines are discussed in Appendix 1, because their influence has been the foundation on which the entire MiG-21 story was based. But the first members of the next generation of MiG-21s, the Ye-9 series, happened to be powered by the R-11 F2S-300 engine, simply because it was available and the R-13 series were not. One has to reflect on the problems facing the people—not in the VVS (air force) nor in the powerful aviation ministry, but in the MiG OKB itself—who had to decide at what points, amidst a profusion of development prototypes, to introduce a new Ye number. The number Ye-9 appears to date from 1968, and reasonably enough it was brought in

*In typical Soviet style, the Ye-9 members are often hard to tell apart, though actually quite different aircraft. This is a MiG-21bis*

*There are no dramatic differences between the cockpits of any series examples of the Ye-9 family, though this is the 'office' of an MF. The constricted space means that many items were pushed into inconvenient locations. Note the bulky HUD sight, radar display and twin seat ejection handles behind the stick*

LEFT
*An early MiG-21PF Type 77 in service with the Indian Air Force. Unlike previous imported MiG-21s the Hindustan-built aircraft have all stencils in English. Note SK-1 seat and vizor*

BELOW
*Another view of an early HAL-built Type 77 (MiG-21PF) of the Indian Air Force, showing the braking-parachute compartment ready to be reloaded. The parachute is normally mandatory, as being cheaper than replacing wheel brakes*

*A beautiful air-to-air study of a MiG-21F-13 of the US Air Force, operating from the Nellis complex (probably Indian Springs AFB). Note the extreme nose-high AOA required to hold formation with what is obviously a fairly slow camera ship. A US VHF/Tacan aerial has been added under the fuselage*

*Egypt has gradually restored most of its MiG-21s to combat status, including this MF seen in 1981 at Al Manzilah AB in the Nile delta area. Several camouflage schemes were then in use. Only now, in 1986, is much Western updating being incorporated (Herman J Sixma, IAAP)*

ABOVE
*A MiG-21US at Al Manzila AB in Egypt's Nile delta in 1981. This particular aircraft has only two missile pylons, but it has an AOA sensor, instructor periscope, blown flaps and broad vertical tail. Service number is 5742 (Herman J Sixma, IAAP)*

ABOVE RIGHT
*Close-up of the nose of the Egyptian MiG-21US, showing the squadron badge. The trainers have flown more hours than most of the Egyptian single-seat MiG-21s, and are certain to go on even after existing Alpha Jet orders are completed (Herman J Sixma, IAAP)*

RIGHT
*An immaculate MiG-21bis of the Finnish* Ilmavoimat *(air force) parked outside the Valmet factory at Tampere. The Finns are quite capable of making MiG-21s but have not even received a license to make spare parts (Herman J Sixma, IAAP)*

ABOVE
*The cruciform braking canopy begins to collapse as speed bleeds off at the end of the landing run of a Finnish MiG-21bis. The Finns seldom fly with weapons (Herman J Sixma, IAAP)*

RIGHT
*Readying a Finnish bis for flight, showing the canopy, q-feel probe and anti-blast fence (which the Finns paint black/yellow) Herman J Sixma, IAAP)*

LEFT
*A Finnish MiG-21bis retracts gear on takeoff. These aircraft appear to have an S-3M RWR system, but lack the Chrome-Nickel installation (Herman J Sixma, IAAP)*

LEFT
*Close-up of the badge of* Ilmavoimat *HävLa 31, in the Karelian Wing. All stencilling throughout the aircraft is in Russian
(Herman J Sixma, IAAP)*

ABOVE
*A portrait at Kuopio-Rissala of MK-143, a MiG-21UM in immaculate condition. The MiG-21 pilots were made green with envy by the visit to their airbase of a team of MiG-29s from Soviet Frontal Aviation in early July 1986. Almost certainly this next-but-one generation MiG will be Finland's MiG-21 replacement
(Jyrki Laukkanen)*

RIGHT
*Close-up of the nose gear of a MiG-21MF visiting France. Note the hydraulic lines to the disc brake and the fact that the entire door area is bulged below the bottom of the fuselage. Just behind the gun can be seen the safety cable linking the blanking plates over the auxiliary suck-in inlet doors*

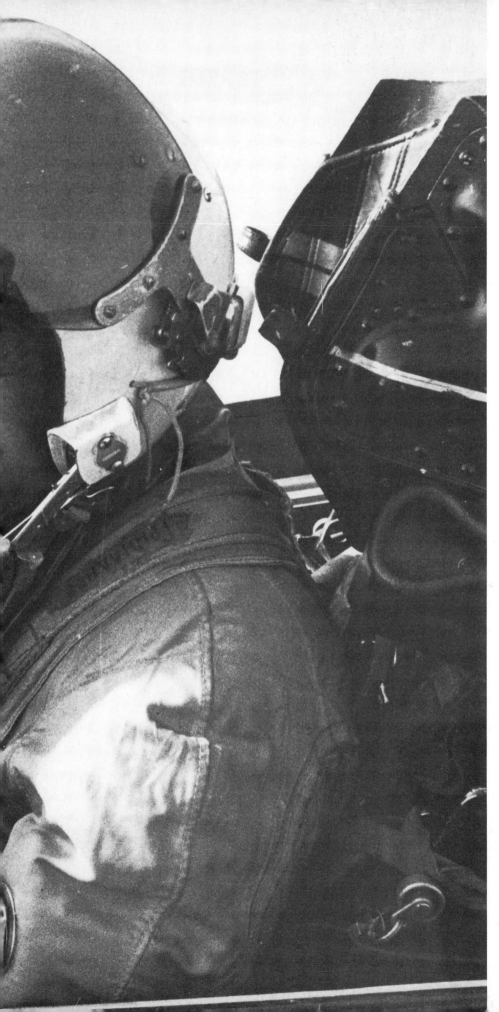

*According to the official caption 'Lt-Col Yu Churilov holds a thumb-up sign appreciating the good readiness of his plane', though his MiG-21bis looks distinctly well used. The lack of space and cluttered view ahead are self-evident (Tass)*

to tie up several improvements which had been flight tested during the preceding 18 months. These included a further increase in volume of the dorsal spine fairing, continued increase in fin chord (introduced with the PFM), a new radar (though fitting into the same aerodynamic envelope), and the addition of two extra wing pylons under the outer wings.

Features continued which had been introduced previously included the sideways-hinged canopy, KM-1 (zero/zero) seat, blown flaps, pitot tube above the inlet (though from now on offset to the right) and provision for the GP-9 gun pack. According to the Indians, this gun pack appeared to rankle with the Soviet negotiators, because it had been introduced only because of Indian pressure. In the Ye-9 provision for this pack was made, as an alternative to a centreline fuel tank, but the author has never seen it in Soviet service. The Ye-9 also at last introduced as standard a feature which had been requested at intervals for at least a decade previously: an Alpha (angle of attack) indicator. This was installed in a way seen on many Soviet aircraft from 1960 onwards, in a standard fit on the left side of the forward fuselage in which AOA is measured by a smooth cylinder at right angles to the airflow, with a streamlined fairing at its nose and tail. This had been requested by top Soviet pilots from the late 1950s onwards, and from about the mid-1960s by Indian and other export pilots. It almost eliminates real problems even in the most serious air combat or in bad-weather landings, though it was to be a further decade before its readings were to appear on a HUD.

One area in which the author has no information concerns any pressure to modify the wing. In his brief chat with Mikoyan in 1969 the author asked whether the Soviet designer was happy with the wing of the MiG-21, which had not changed at all (apart from switching to blown flaps) in about 15 years. The answer was simply in the affirmative, and certainly there has not been much alteration in this wing in the subsequent 15 years, which takes us to the end of MiG-21 production. The author has been unable to find evidence to support the statement by one Western writer that the fatigue life of the wing is 'equal to two years' normal operation'. Some Indian and Egyptian aircraft have exceeded 3,000 hours in more than ten years.

On the other hand, there have been several first-hand pilot reports which criticise the MiG-21 for the very firm, almost violent, change of trim on lowering full blown flap. As discussed earlier, the aircraft, held with stick loose and centred, balloons at least 200 m (656 ft) upwards and then sinks very rapidly, at a rate

*Right side of the cockpit of a MiG-21MF, showing the battery of radio, navaid and EW switches on the right wall and the massive ejection-seat handles*

This photograph of the left main landing gear leads off a
series of detail illustrations of two MiG-21MF aircraft
(4411 and 4412) which visited France in 1978. No
annotation is offered on this particular view because all
items are covered elsewhere. It will be noted, however, that
the inboard pylons were removed for this visit. A soft
mattress covers the inboard upper wing surface

Detail of the MF's left main landing-gear bay area: *1, drop tank suspension lock; 2, Fuel Tank No 3; 3, '4412'. the individual aircraft number repeated on many parts of the airframe; 4, pressure warning; 5, oxygen cylinders for high-altitude engine start; 6, landing light (retracted); 7, tank drain; 8, oil tank access; 9, Pump 495; 10, ground electrical power socket; 11, disconnection cone; 12, rocket thrust bracket; 13, rear airbrake (part open)*

*Another left main-gear close-up, items not annotated being covered on the previous page: 1, gun gas overboard vents; 2, pylon adjustment instructions; 3, tank group sump; 4, drain valve; 5, fuel tank drainage control; 6, ARU-3V navaid; 7, inboard pylon location; 8, S-3ZM RWR forward-sector receiver; 9, trestle point; 10, engine mount; 11, SPS flap cylinder; 12, RV flap valve; 13, rocket rear attachment; 14, engine gearbox; 15, engine hydraulic group; 16, airbrake closed; 17, '4411'; 18, tank pylon*

*View from above the left wing of No 4412: 1, line safety valve and overboard vent; 2, ARU-3V; 3, charging mechanism; 4, directions for disconnection of rear fuselage; 5, '4412'; 6, SPS blown flaps control access; 7, temperature control; 8, Chrome-nickel EW receiver; 9, navigation light; 10, store loading instructions; 11, integral tank boundary; 12, hinged flap fairing; 13, RV-UM altimeter aerial*

which calls for experience if it is to be arrested before touchdown. Not being privy to the in-fighting, it seems to the author that the Soviet Union fell into the silly but common situation in which the experienced pilots said 'There's no problem, what are these young idiots complaining about?' From the early 1970s the AOA readout has at least helped pilots to get the landing right, making a firm touchdown on all three wheels at once yet without breaking the landing gears.

The one obvious distinguishing feature of the Ye-9 family is the enlarged dorsal fairing joining the canopy to the fin, and it is this which brought many sub-variants into this group even though they retained the F2S-300 engine. The immediate reaction of Western analysts to the enlarged fairing was that it had been introduced in order to increase internal fuel capacity, though a little thought would have shown this to be unlikely. Mikoyan and, especially, chief designer R A Belyakov (who

*Not forming part of the detail close-up series, this photo was taken at Moscow Kubinka on 17 March 1972 and shows the C-in-C of the Swedish Flygvapen (air force), Gen Stig Karl Nuren, seated in a MiG-21MF. Assisting is Col-Gen of Aviation A N Yefimov, 1st Deputy C-in-C of the VVS*

succeeded Mikoyan as OKB head on Mikoyan's death four years later in 1970), had long since been aware of the need for greater engine power to meet inevitable growth in weight. Tumanskii had of his own volition started the R-13 programme in the late 1950s, following soon afterwards with the totally 'clean sheet of paper' R-25, and he assured the MiG team there was no need to worry in the longer term. But there was never any question of accepting any appreciable weight growth prior to the availability of the R-13.

Thus, the big dorsal fairing was introduced purely for aerodynamic reasons. One of the meaningful replies given by Mikoyan to the author was 'Da',

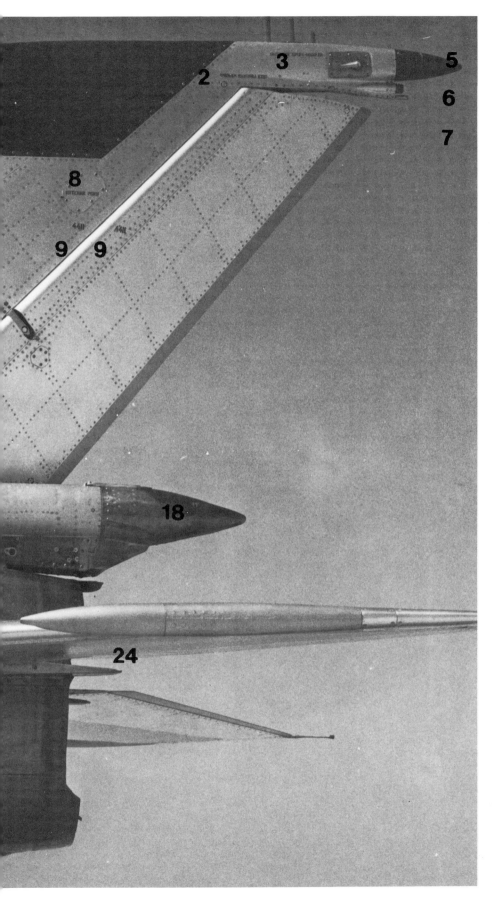

Detail view of left side of tail of MiG-21MF No 4411:1, attachments for wire aerial (internal); 2, SOD transponder filter aerial; 3; SRZO-2 IFF aerial; 4, aerial Chrome-Nickel EW system; 5, dielectric fairing; 6, navigation light; 7, fuel vent; 8, RSIU-5 aerial; 9, '4411'; 10, S-3M RWR aft sector receivers on compass magnetometer fairing; 11, booster N12-51; 12, rack 107; 13, pumping group NP-27 (tailplane power unit); 14, cable attachment for removing fin; 15 (twice) rudder power unit; 16, cooling inlet; 17, air-system throttle; 18, braking-parachute doors; 19, 'before undocking fuselage check tailplane is leading-edge down'; 20, hydraulic pipe fairing; 21, afterburner attachment inner chamber; 22, tailplane crank fairing; 23, nozzle actuator cylinder; 24, tailplane anti-flutter weight

**ABOVE**
*Entente cordiale at Kubinka, in Moscow Military District, as French Normandie-Niemen pilot Jean-Pierre Job (right) hits it off with opposite number MiG-21 jock Vladimir Petrov on 28 July 1977 (Tass)*

**LEFT**
*Urgent departure of a PFM with a.t.o. rockets; flaps are not used (Aviation Magazine, via William Green)*

**UPPER RIGHT**
*A Czech MiG-21MF with three tanks, a ferry configuration (Miroslav Balous via Pilot Press)*

**RIGHT**
*Arrival with airbrake of a CL (Czech) MF*

*This PFMA, basically an MF but without gun, wore red 'invasion stripes' for the swift takeover of Prague to quell the move towards democracy on 21 August 1968*

*Just beginning its takeoff run, this MiG-21 MF of the Yugoslav air force is about to ignite its afterburner. The electronic fit is simpler than on VVS aircraft (Robert J Ruffle archives)*

ABOVE
*For comparative purposes with the picture below left, this is another Yugoslav PF. All Yugoslav PFs had the GP-9 gun pack, there being no internal gun provided*

BELOW
*Floodlit No 22811 of the Yugoslav air force, a standard MiG-21MF, on tow along a taxiway. The massive canvas drapes on the boom and nose suggest imperfect weathering*

when asked whether the drag figures for the 'MF' series were better than those for the 'PF' (at that time the author knew nothing of the later Ye numbers). Pressed further on application of the area rule, and precisely why the drag was lower, Mikoyan took refuge in unhelpful replies, such as 'We designed it correctly'. Just looking at the two shapes it is obvious that, while the body volume of the Ye-9 is greater, the nose-to-tail plot of cross-section areas forms a smooth (probably perfectly optimized) curve, whereas the lower curve of the Ye-7s is kinked. Indeed, the Japanese magazine *Aireview* has published a sketch suggesting that the Ye-7s actually have a greater cross-section immediately downstream of the cockpit, giving a bulge followed by a waist. In the absence of official drawings this is hard to confirm; the author has been unable to obtain an opinion. A senior official of HAL said 'Very few of the parts in the upper fuselage of the Type 88 are the same as those of the Type 77. The canopy is different, as is all the structure immediately behind. The later version did not simply continue from the point of maximum cross-section but was redesigned all the way back from the windscreen.'

The enlarged fairing is made up of removable light-alloy sections removable after undoing countersunk screws. This gives access to the interior, which differs only in small details from that of the PF and other Ye-7 versions. The bigger fairing curves smoothly into the fin, which in effect is slightly reduced in area. The tailplane power unit in the fin, and its control input, were unchanged. So were the braking parachute installation downstream.

By the mid-1960s the SPS blown flap had firmly established itself as superior, and it has remained on all subsequent MiG-21 versions. Unlike the original track-mounted flap, the SPS flap can be used to reduce turn radius in combat, the pilot having to move it manually to the takeoff setting. The flaps are stressed for use at high IAS, and beyond a certain dynamic pressure (equivalent to about 420 km/h at sea level or 550 km/h at 20,000 ft) begin to close by themselves. This has always been regarded as an important combat bonus, because having selected flap the pilot can ignore it if he wishes to accelerate, knowing that it will not continue to degrade his energy state.

Structurally the wing of the Ye-9 series is almost identical to previous types. Very little local reinforcement was needed to install the outboard pylons, and these were also found to have less than the predicted extra drag. The total added mass, including pylon and AAM interface shoe, is limited to 220.5 lb (100 kg). These pylons are used for AAMs only, though presumably they could be fitted with ejector racks for other stores of similar weight.

Numerous internal system changes were introduced, some of them resulting in a very small reduction in fuel capacity. By far the most important

was a change in type of radar. The replacement set, which was probably designed in 1959–63, had to fit into the same places as the original R1L, and in particular the mechanically steered antenna had to fit into the existing inlet centrebody. Called 'Jay Bird' by NATO, the second-generation radar has no kinship with the R1L, and operates in J band at 12,800–13,200 MHz, with PRFs of 1,592/1,792, 2,042/2,048 and 2,716/2,724. Peak power has been estimated at 100 kW, though there is evidence that it is slightly greater, and it has a CW mode providing a guidance beam for the so-called 'AA-2-2 Advanced Atoll' AAM, which is generally similar to the original missile apart from having semi-active radar guidance.

Though a major improvement in transmitter power (and hence range and performance against ECM) over the R1L, and especially in its ability to give clear target information at quite low altitudes,

*As proclaimed on the nose, Indian Air Force No C1532*
*was the first MiG-21M to be completed by Hindustan*
*Aeronautics. It is seen at the Nasik plant, about to taxi*
*out for its maiden flight*

operational shortcoming to have no choice.

Since 1979 introduction of the totally new AAM known to NATO as 'AA-8 Aphid' has opened out launch parameters greatly, and also enabled successful kills to be made from slightly greater range, despite the much smaller size of the new missile. This new weapon is said to have demonstrated very high lethality in its IR-homing version, even against aircraft at the lowest possible level. There is still an ongoing need for a modern look-down radar for the MiG-21, with the ability to provide reliable guidance for radar-homing missiles against low-altitude targets. According to various Western electronics companies no such radar has ever been forthcoming, showing that in the Soviet procurement plan the MiG-21 development ended with the known versions, and earlier than 1970.

Probably the first production fighter in the Ye-9 family was the MiG-21MA, which appears to have entered production in 1965. The Indian designation of Type 88 is puzzling, but then no sense can easily be made of several other airframe type numbers in the MiG-21 family tree. Certainly the slick assumption that Ye-6, -7 and -9 derivatives have type numbers which begin with 6, 7 or 9 respectively is unwarranted, logical as the Soviets may be. Had he known the situation the author would certainly have sought elucidation from Mikoyan, and in due course all is likely to be revealed. Fortunately for sanity the next production model to appear, which was a reconnaissance variant, bore the airframe type number of 94, which is what one might have expected (thinks: but why was the Ye-8 STOL with lift jets the 92?).

Introduction of a reconnaissance version at this juncture was logical. With the F2S-300 engine and higher weights the first members of the Ye-9 family were less agile than their predecessors, which tended to negate their other advantages as fighters. On the other hand with lower aerodynamic drag they could actually work up to fractionally higher speeds on the level in the clean condition, so the 94 was not unexpected, receiving the basic variant designation MiG-21R. In fact this was the first of at least three R versions, and the key feature at the start was carriage of a camera pod on the centreline. Curiously this pod has often been described as 'slipper type', but in fact its cross-section is roughly a flat-bottomed circle and it is carried well below the fuselage on a faired-in pylon. The normal sensor fit was originally either five or six cameras, such as one forward oblique, two or three overlapping vertical and at least one panoramic camera giving horizon-to-horizon coverage.

This neat pod, whose drag was less than that of a UV-16-57 rocket pod (hardly surprising), weighed approximately 1,100 lb (500 kg) and was linked to the aircraft's navigation system and radar altimeter. Means were provided to print out data on each exposure; the information would probably consist of either a map reference or lat/long, plus date and time

the new radar still suffered from rather short useful ranges and lack of true look-down capability against targets at extremely low level. Several user air forces have said that against typical fighter targets it is rare to acquire at ranges greater than 30 km (19 miles), and only one target can be handled at a time. Of course, the enemy aircraft must be illuminated all the time until the AAM hits (or fails to), and as the missile has a very short range anyway—roughly 4 miles, 6.5 km—this forces the MiG-21 to close right in among what may be a large formation of hostile fighters. This might be its pilot's intention anyway, because all MiG-21s have been designed to 'mix it', but it is an

*Included in this lineup at an Indian Air Force base are MiG-21Ms (Type 96) Nos C1476, 1491, 1507, 1501, 1531, 1493 and 1504. The nearest, 1476, bears the legend 'Rupees 127 crores'. As a crore is ten million, this seems quite a lot of money; maybe the four UV-16-57 launchers are thrown in*

143

Another view of the same lineup (see previous page). The location is given a 'an advanced fighter base in the Punjab'

ABOVE
Two MiG-21Ms, Type 96, over rugged terrain facing Pakistan. The aircraft are C1521 and C1497, flying with Indian Air Force No 7 Squadron, 'Battle Axes', whose black and yellow emblem can be seen on the nose. The Type 96 was issued to 19 IAF squadrons. There has been much variation in IAF camouflage, but for most of their life these fighters have been medium grey and dark green

RIGHT
Another view, perhaps as seen by an enemy, of C1521 and C1497 flying amongst the mountains. Their drop tanks are Indian-built

OVERLEAF
An evocative 'mood picture' of domestic chores on the flightline of No 7 'Battle Axes' Squadron, IAF. Some Type 96 fighters had not been camouflaged when this picture was taken, and camouflage has not been applied to the Type 66 trainers such as U2146. Note the An-12BP climbing smokily away

144

The MiG-21bis, known as Type 76 but not referred to as
such by Hindustan Aeronautics, succeeded the Type 96 on
the Nasik line in 1980, and a reported 220 will have been
assembled at completion in early 1987. All IAF fighters
have been dramatically upgraded in capability by equipping
them with the French Matra 550 Magic and Soviet (and
later HAL-built) R-60 (Aphid) advanced dogfight missiles

and possibly altitude. Some Western reports (eg *Air Enthusiast* May 1974) stated that this pod combined cameras plus fuel, but the author can say with assurance that no such fuel-plus-sensor pod had been carried by the MiG-21 up to 1983, and it is unlikely that one has appeared since. There have, however, been several other reconnaissance versions of MiG-21.

Historically the earliest installation of reconnaissance sensors goes back to about 1963, on a MiG-21F development prototype. This comprised a pallet on which were shock-mounted three cameras, one forward oblique, one panoramic and one vertical framing camera. This filled almost the whole space under the cockpit floor, and made it impossible to install any guns, but it had the advantages of being easily removed and having little effect on weight or drag, and none on internal fuel. So far as is known this installation was not adopted by Warsaw Pact forces,

*C2103, an HAL-assembled MiG-21bis, is seen in air-superiority grey which may be retroactively applied to earlier IAF MiG fighters*

but in 1979 it was realized that it was a common fit on export MiG-21s, notably in Egypt. British photographer Denis Hughes visited many units of the Egyptian AF in late 1981, bringing back the first good pictures of Ye-9 versions based on the PFMA and simply known as the MiG-21R. These had the same old three-camera pallet, but in a permanent installation. In this case the whole pallet hinges open along the right side, exposing the cameras for servicing or reloading. Another feature which was not recognised until later was a new RHAWS (radar homing and warning system) with its passive receivers in small streamlined pods at the wingtips.

Unlike the common SO-69 Sirena series of passive RWR (radar warning receiver) installations, these tip pods have larger spiral helix antennas at front and rear giving 360° coverage in the horizontal plane and limited reception from below. These pods have not been seen on any other MiG-21 sub-type.

Yet another of the many pods carried by these late/middle-period MiG-21s is an Elint sensor. First seen on an aircraft of the PWL (Polish air force), this packages a totally new set of sensors into the same metal pod as used by the commonest centreline reconnaissance pod. Front and rear windows are cut in each side through which the receivers for the groups of wavebands can pick up signals, the apertures being skinned over with glassfibre. Information is recorded within the pod, which has only a simple electric power connection to the aircraft. So far as is known the obvious conversion of surplus older MiG-21 fighters into dedicated Elint or ECM platforms has not taken place, though the author suspects this is merely a matter of time.

By 1967 the designation MiG-21M had been authorized to cover a group of improvements which, in practice, were introduced to production as they became available. This means that many aircraft received the M (Type 96) designation but were not completed to this build-standard. The most important new feature, and the one which even Mikoyan admitted had needed considerable development effort, was the internal gun.

Whereas in the early 1960s the Soviet Aviation Ministry had given the Indians the strong impression they were being difficult and foolish to want a gun, by 1967 US Air Force experience in Vietnam had resulted in a complete about-face. The MiG OKB was instructed to fit the GSh-23L twin-barrel gun into the MiG-21 itself, not merely into the GP-9 gondola which then had to be hung externally. The task was far from simple. Fitting the gun was the easy part, though steel skin was needed under the fuselage near the muzzles. The difficulty was where to put the ammunition. Many schemes were tried, some of them affecting the aircraft's external appearance, before it was decided to wrap the 200-round ammunition belt right round the centre fuselage, round the central inlet duct. Reloading has to be done through a single removable panel on the left, and, as the armourer cannot get more than his arms through, it needs a fair amount of skill to complete the task quickly. The belt is already the correct length and made up with rounds in the correct sequence. One end is fed down to the bottom of the left side of the magazine compartment and laid layer on layer until the top almost blocks off the aperture. The other end

*The pilot gets aboard an IAF MiG-21bis while a ground crewman waits with his bonedome helmet. The aircraft is air superiority grey, but the taxiway is camouflaged*

*Though often seen, no apology is needed for including this example from a series of photographs taken during Western visits in 1978 by a picked MiG-21bis team (Klaus Niska via Robert J Ruffle)*

**LEFT**
*MiG-21bis commemorating the 17th Congress of the Leninist Young Communist League of the SU (Robert J Ruffle archives)*

*Typical armament of a MiG-21bis in the air combat role is one GSh-23L gun, two or four R-60 (AA-8 Aphid) missiles and two AA-2-2 Advanced Atoll missiles, the latter requiring target illumination by the Jay Bird radar*

*Gears begin to tuck away as a vic of MiG-21bis fighters scramble. The formation is quite tight, and No 55 is having to use airbrake. The other two aircraft bear the 'standard of excellence' badge. Nos 53 and 55 are equipped with ILS (small aerials below nose and above fin)*

LEFT
*A rather loose flypast by MiG-21MFs visiting Reims, France, in 1978. As noted previously the inboard pylons were removed from these aircraft. Steel skin ahead of the gun muzzles appears dark*

TOP
*The windscreen rear frame (and front of the canopy) of the bis is more acutely sloped than in earlier versions. This bis has UV-16-57 pods*

ABOVE
*No 54 is a bis equipped with ILS (NATO name Swift Rod) at nose and tail. Most of it is painted air-superiority grey*
*(Robert J Ruffle archives)*

*Another ILS-equipped MiG-21bis, with sunlight coming
from an angle which emphasizes the area ruled curves and
wheel bulge of the centre fuselage
(Robert J Ruffle archives)*

is then fed in and pushed round until a colleague
under the aircraft can insert it into the right side of the
gun. The rest of the belt is then fed in blindly to fill
the right side of the magazine. Cases from the two
breeches are expelled overboard via short pipes
which slope down to left and right at the rear
sufficiently to avoid any impacts on the rear airbrake.
Links are shot up an internal duct into a collector.
The whole gun compartment is ventilated by two
prominent ram-air inlets on the underside.

Fitting the internal gun required another modification. The muzzles are close to the auxiliary inlet
doors, and to prevent disturbance to the engine
airflow small horizontal fences were fitted beneath
these doors. A fair amount of tinkering was needed to
get these seemingly simple fences right, doing their
job and without the wake at high AOA adversely
affecting flow over the wing roots. Almost without
exception Western reports describe these fences as
being FOD deflectors, whereas in fact the ground is
the one place they are not needed!

Another feature of the Ye-96 was a rear-view
mirror in the top of the canopy. It is surprising that
this had not appeared before; indeed a few export PFs
had earlier been fitted with internal mirrors, but these
interfered with the already rather poor forward
vision. The new pattern is basically a square vertical
mirror which fits inside a cast aluminium frame
screwed into the top of the canopy, some of the frames
having an elongated tail.

At some point in the development the MiG OKB

undertook a careful structural revision, because
weight had grown in almost every one of the
preceding ten years. In any case, there was
considerable pressure (one suspects, led by the export
customers who are better able to speak their mind) for
restoration of the fuel lost to the ammunition bay, and
this threatened a further major increase. Most of the
structural changes were minor, and certainly the total
increase in structure weight was of little consequence,
but while they were doing the job the structural
designers went the whole hog and cleared the MiG-
21 for operaration at significantly increased indicated
airspeeds. Earlier variants were held to a manoeuvre
factor of 6G at IAS of 1000 km/h, making the aircraft
subsonic up to about 13,000 ft (4 km). In contrast the
structure of the M, and this really means the wing,
was cleared for supersonic flight at all altitudes, the
limit at sea level being 1300 km/h (808 mph), or about
Mach 1.06. In practice, it appears that export
customers, including Egypt and India, do not exceed
660 knots IAS, a sea-level Mach equivalent of 1
exactly.

To recap, the aforementioned design changes were
all combined in the initial Ye-9 production series,

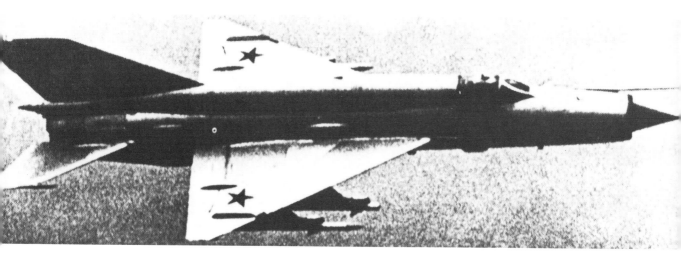

**TOP**
*Certainly the best photograph so far available showing MiG-21 missile armament, this bis is carrying R-60 (AA-8 Aphid) advanced dogfight AAMs on the inboard pylons and AA-2-2 Advanced Atoll semi-active radar AAMs outboard (note the latter's long noses). Landing light is on*

**ABOVE**
*Apart from showing the rather scarce MiG-21SMB (widely reported as the SMT), this affords a direct comparison between the K-13A (AA-2 Atoll) IR-homing missile (inboard) and the longer AA-2-2 Advanced Atoll radar-homing weapon outboard*
*(Robert J Ruffle archives)*

ABOVE
One of a limited number of clear photographs of the
humpbacked SMB version, this shows an example from a
Frontal Aviation regiment wearing the 'standard of
excellence' badge on the nose. Note how the bulged spine
fairing extends right across the vertical tail
(Flug Revue)

BELOW
One of the 30 new MiG-21bis fighters purchased from the
Soviet Union by Finland's Ilmavoimat (air force) taxying
in at Kuopio-Rissala. Large sections at the rear are
unpainted
(Veikko Timonen via Robert F Dorr)

MiG-21bis fighters of the Ilmavoimat parked at Kuopio-
Rissala. Their unit is HavLv 31, in the Karjalan Lennosto
(Karelian Wing)
(Veikko Timonen via Robert F Dorr)

originally designated PFMA in the Soviet Union but later simplified to MiG-21MA, which is widely said to have been the export designation for the same aircraft. At least 2,000 aircraft, including reconnaissance versions, were built to this standard in 1967–70 in the Soviet Union, and (three only) in India in 1973. By 1970 the R-13 engine was at last available, and this was considered very important to combat the growth in weight. With the new engine the designation was changed to Ye-96, with service designation MiG-21MF.

The R-13 was not a fresh design but a careful revision of the R-11 with major changes in internal aerodynamics and materials. The former increased mass flow at takeoff rpm by 18 per cent, while switching from steel to titanium in the LP compressor blades and case, and in certain other parts, actually reduced dry weight by over 110 lb (50 kg). The engine KB were also clearly more confident (and in fact were proud of this engine) because it was soon authorized to run 300 hours between overhauls, compared with 250 for the much 'more experienced' F2S-300.

With this significantly more powerful engine the performance was in most respects even higher than that of the original Ye-6 series and MiG-21F, and noticeably superior to that of the early Ye-9 variants. Predictably, this relaxation of pressure on keeping down weight was immediately put to use—just as, when a commercial transport is given more power or more lift, to improve STOL performance, the customers instantly translate this into greater masses of fuel or payload!

In the case of the MiG-21 the result was a new sub-type in which the fuel removed from the Type 96 (M/MF) was replaced. The only place to put it was in the dorsal spine, much of which had been a mere aerodynamic shape. Most of the spine's length had to remain full of nothing but control runs, piping, basic electrics and avionics, and similar auxiliaries. To get in the required amount of fuel within a single short (0.95 m, 37.5 in) length the spine had to be again enlarged; indeed it was more than doubled in cross-section compared with the Type 96. This was no problem at all. Tunnel testing showed that a properly area-ruled spine with the required cross-section would make hardly any difference to drag, and (this was a bigger worry) would not adversely affect airflow past the vertical tail.

There seems to be some confusion about the resulting aircraft. Western reports consistently give its designation as SMT, but the Russians are not noted for using English (T for tank), and there is much evidence the actual designation is SMB (B for bak, tank). Apart from making the fighter look a trifle hump-backed it even enhanced its appearance (in the author's opinion). Apart from the much bigger cross-section of what has been called a saddle, rather than a spine, the longer-range model is immediately identified by the way the spine is so wide it has to

continue right across the broad fin to merge into the drag-chute tube at the rear. Of course the extra fuel, weighing 1,000 lb (454 kg), is located well aft of the centre of gravity, and destabilizes the aircraft. Pilots say that there is no problem. With the size of tail surfaces combined with the advanced flight-control and autostabilization system, fed with AOA and with pitch/yaw signals from the nose instrument boom, the destabilization cannot cause excursions beyond the safe flight envelope. In theory it ought to make this variant into a superior dogfighter, though the author has been unable to find confirmation of this.

The author has never met R A Belyakov, present head of the MiG OKB, and does not know whether the 'SMT' was ever planned as the definitive production MiG-21. In the event it proved to be a rather scarce interim aircraft which merely led to what actually was the final version, called MiG-21bis. The Soviet Union has for almost 60 years used the Latin suffix bis (two, twice, or more precisely an encore) to indicate what in former years Britain might have called 'Mk 2'. In the case of the MiG-21 the bis is more like 'Mk 22', and it has been adopted (so Russians have seriously suggested) because the programme had run out of ordinary suffix letters!

Superficially the bis looks like an 'SMT' that has tried to lose weight. In practice it is the biggest modification in the entire MiG-21 family, affecting structure, systems and powerplant. The airframe was for the second time subjected to extensive revision to improve structural efficiency throughout. In going from the original Ye-9 to the production Ye-96 the objective had been to introduce local reinforcement, or increases in gauge of webs and skin, to permit safe operation at greater weights and higher IAS. With the bis the decision was taken almost to start again and come up with a better structure than the end-product of almost 20 years of modifications. By the 1970s fighters were expected to have service lives several times longer than they were in the 1950s, and this made fatigue, and the accumulation of local damage, an important new factor. In the bis the structure was revised both to seek better solutions, by wrapping a new skeleton round what had become a different aircraft as far as systems and equipment are concerned, and also to give a long troublefree life. The author can vouch for a lot of this, visible on close walkround inspection, but the only thing that looks different from the MF from a distance is the upper mainwheel blister on each side! Closer study shows that, in fact, the entire spine, or saddle fairing, has been yet again redesigned. This time it was fully optimized for minimum drag, the interior having been replanned to devote a much greater proportion

*A Sidewinder streaks away, almost certainly (at this distance) locked-on to the MiG-21 of the North Vietnamese People's air force seen on the right. Note the pale rings of the gunsight graticule. No information on launch aircraft or date (via Paul F Crickmore)*

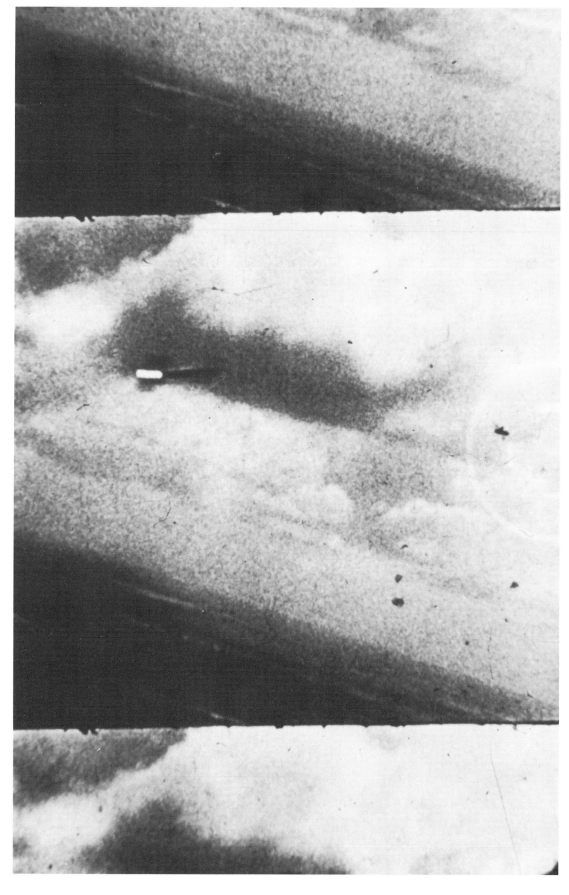

*Contrasting* Ilmavoimat *(Finnish AF) types seen together
at the Utti airbase airshow on 17 May 1981
(Veikko Timonen via Robert F Dorr)*

of its length to fuel. Total internal capacity is only slightly increased over that of the 'SMT', but the cross-section area is brought back close to that of the MF, but with a subtly different profile which increases the available internal volume. So far as the author knows, and despite several Western drawings, all bis versions have a clear MF-type break between the spine and the parachute container.

The second advance in the bis, about which less is known, is that the mission avionics are upgraded. Even the Ye-96 series were rudimentary aircraft by the standards of the 1970s, little different in concept from fighters of the Korean War era. With the bis it was accepted that much more had to be done, especially in navigation and weapon delivery in the air-to-ground mission. The author has no 'inside information' on the resulting equipment fit, but as no doppler is fitted it would be reasonable to suppose that an inertial system is now installed. The radar is probably still a 'Jay Bird' or close relative, and there is no evidence of a FLIR, laser or any other sensor. The reports of upgraded avionics must therefore refer chiefly to communications and to EW installations such as the RWR and possibly ECM. In 1970–75 a major effort was made to develop a whole new generation of EW installations for the Tu-22M and for various helicopters, later models of Su-24 and the completely new MiG-29 and MiG-31 and Su-25 and -27. It is highly likely that some of the simpler RWR receivers, analysers and displays have also been adapted to the MiG-21bis, though there is no evidence of any chaff/flare dispenser or active jammer carried internally. Still with only five pylons, external jammers inevitably cut into the options for tanks and ordnance.

The third advance in the bis is yet another new engine. As with most things Soviet there are puzzles. Many years ago the author was led to believe that Tumanskii's known 'new generation engine' was being developed for 'a new tactical attack aircraft', and putting two and two together this seemed to be the Su-25 (what else?). Yet all recent reports have consistently stated that this highly subsonic machine is powered by two old R-13s (according to *Jane's*, R-13-300s, though obviously they are without afterburners). The same authoritative annual gives the engines of the Su-21 (or Su-15) 'Flagon' as 'two R-13F2-300s, each rated at 15,875 lb with afterburning', despite the fact that no such engine has appeared on a MiG-21. The cause for surprise is that, whereas presumably the MiG-21bis could simply have had this F2-300 version of its existing engine bolted in, the trouble was taken to qualify it with a totally new engine which, despite reports to the contrary, did need some engine-bay redesign as well as a fair amount of change to the fuel and control systems.

This new engine is the R-25. As it seems to have no application apart from the MiG-21bis, what was the 'new tactical attack aircraft'? Moreover, profligate as the Soviet Union certainly is with arms funding, it

seems unlikely that the Tumanskii KB should have been required to design and qualify a 'clean sheet of paper' engine merely to power the final batches of a fast-obsolescing fighter. Be that as it may, the R-25 is a very big advance over the R-11 and R-13, as explained in Appendix 1. Tumanskii's gifted team greatly increased the mass flow and pressure ratio, kept down the weight, reduced the total parts-count and made the R-25 almost installationally interchangeable with the R-13-300. There remain unanswered questions. It seems self-evident that the nose inlet and duct must have been enlarged, but this has not been reported and is certainly not obvious. Second, how did the MiG OKB get the engine into the space available seeing that underneath the enlarged engine inlet is an accessory group at least as deep as that of the R-13?

From the pilot's viewpoint the R-25 dramatically raises performance of the bis well above anything attained by any previous model, despite further modest increase in weights. Another very important feature is that the engine has a completely new afterburner, which lights up 'softly' (without a sudden bang and jerk) and burns in two distinct zones, lit in succession even on slam accelerations. This afterburner is the key factor in a very large improvement in all-round performance at high altitude, an area where earlier MiG-21s were rated poor. The new afterburner was designed primarily for use in high-altitude air combat, rather than for takeoff, and a further very big advantage is that the rather clumsy mechanical detent lock in the cockpit engine control is eliminated. The bis has a plain single throttle lever giving smooth control of thrust from idling to maximum afterburner.

The final point to reiterate is that these improvements did not happen all at once. Several supposedly authoritative Eastern and Western documents report the MiG-21bis (called Fishbed L by NATO), followed by the MiG-21Mbis (called Fishbed N). Side elevations published by General Dynamics show the Mbis as having an extra forward-pointing probe or rod under the nose, interpreted by the author as being the usual ILS antenna (NATO name Swift Rod), not used on previous MiG-21 versions and obviously a great help in recovering to base in poor visibility. *Jane's* merely described Fishbed N as having the R-25 engine, and oddly also states 'Further improvement of avionics indicated by 'bow and arrow' antenna on nose' which is a strange description of Swift Rod.

In due course all may be made clear. Meanwhile, to show that the world is probably upside-down, while the factories in the Soviet Union have certainly at last ceased building MiG-21s, and the MiG-21bis (confusingly called Type 75 in some reports) is to cease coming off the HAL line at Nasik at about the time this book appears, the oldest version of all (albeit in a shiny and attractive new form) continues to be made in the time warp of China (Chapter 10).

# Chapter 9
# The U-series

One of the enduring debates of military aviation revolves around the validity of the two-seat dual-control trainer version of the single-seat fighter. What is not widely known is that the first country to standardize such conversions was the Soviet Union, in 1934. Ever since, it has been almost universal Soviet practice to build UTI (instructional trainer fighter) conversions, and the MiG-21 was no exception. (In parentheses, it has been RAF policy as well, but the Tornado was the very first time the trainer had arrived in time to train the pilots).

The Ye-6U trainer prototype first flew in April or May 1960. It had taken rather a long time to emerge, and the airframe standard was that of the original Ye-6, rather than the then-current 21F series fighter. The fuselage was an almost complete redesign, though the most obvious feature was the instructor cockpit added behind the original cockpit, both being covered by separate canopies hinged to the right, and with stays to prop them open linked to the tops of the forward windshield and the second equally massive windshield in front of the instructor. Both seats were at the same level, and the instructor's view was generally poor, especially ahead. The one advanced feature was that KM-1 seats were fitted, for the first time in a MiG-21.

The second cockpit required major revison of both the fuselage tankage and the engine duct, but redesign of the lower part of the fuselage enabled the penalty in fuel to be minimized. When the initial production MiG-21UTI came off the line, probably in January 1963, its internal fuel capacity was 2400 lit, actually a shade more than the usable capacity in the first F-series fighters! The main reason was elimination of the guns and their bulky magazines, but another factor was that the forward airbrakes were replaced by a single brake on the ventral centreline. Retardation with full airbrake resembles fighter versions because the trainers are lighter.

*A revealing picture showing an early PF and a MiG-21U with tail removed for an engine change and seats removed. It has an AOA vane but only two pylons and no periscope* (Aviatsiya i Kosmonavtika)

Rather surprisingly
dressed in full pressure
helmets and anti-G suits,
instructors and pupils are
either trying to sweat off a
few kilos or practising a
combat scramble. Key: 1,
main landing gear door; 2,
tank pylon; 3, skin
covering absent gun bulge;
4, 'specialist under-
fuselage attachment'; 5,
'electrical disconnect 128,
pylon BP3-66-21M'; 6,
airbrake (part open); 7,
root attachment fairing; 8,
handle for inlet blanking
plate (left/right plates bear
aircraft number and are
tied by cable); 9, pitot
probe for q-feel subsystem
(Tass)

173

Many other features were those of the PF, notably including the vertical tail and the long instrument boom mounted above the nose. Less obvious, but equally important, the landing gear was also that of the PF, with enlarged main tyres and high-capacity brakes. 'Odd Rods' IFF was almost the only avionics item fitted apart from communications radio, and the only external store normally carried was the 490-lit centreline tank. Wing pylons were fitted, but seldom used. The UTI's role was pure conversion to type.

Probably only a small number of the UTI were built, though a few were supplied to India as the Type 66-400. The main production of trainers began in 1964 with the MiG-21U. Known as the Type 66 (Ye-66), this introduced the broad vertical tail of the PFM and M, giving generally improved stability and handling. With the new tail came the cross-type braking parachute housed in a tube at the base of the rudder. The Indian Air Force received 42 of this type from Soviet production, with designation Type 66-600 (also known operationally as the MiG-21U Advanced).

In 1965, roughly in parallel with the MiG-21PFS, blown flaps were introduced on the MiG-21US, Type 68. These were generally felt to be unnecessary on the trainer, except for teaching their correct usage on the fighter. Landing run on a good runway with full blowing is 400 m (1,320 ft), though as noted earlier such landings are not normally permitted by ordinary regimental pilots. Along with the SPS flaps came a much-needed periscope for the instructor. Typically crude and effective, it consists of two mirrors pivoted to a new metal roof to the rear canopy. When the landing gear is down, the mirrors are pivoted open to give a zig-zag view ahead. After takeoff, selection of gear up triggers an electrical relay which by a system of push/pull rods folds the internal mirror into its stowed position on the inside of the roof, while the external mirror folds forward and down flush with the top of the canopy.

The puzzling designation of Ye-33 was applied to one or more unidentified types of MiG-21U used to establish women's records. On 22 May 1965 a Ye-33 was used by Natalya Prokhanova to reach a zoom altitude of 24,336 m. On 23 June 1965 Lydia Zaitseva held a sustained altitude of 19,020 m.

Fourth and last of the trainers, the UM, Type 69, has the more powerful R-13-300 engine. This also has other improvements including the four-pylon wing, AOA sensor on the left side of the nose and pitch/yaw sensor vanes on the nose boom. Of course, the demarcation lines between sub-types are not clear-cut, and trainers have been seen with just some, but not all, of the later features. The Soviet VVS appears to have had few, if any, with the instructor periscope until about 1979, though this device is common in other Warsaw Pact air forces. At least one Soviet two-seater has Spin Scan or Jay Bird radar, while perhaps the most interesting of all are the Egyptian US trainers with locally designed belly

pods made at the Air Force factories at Helwan to teach electronic warfare techniques.

In late 1981 the magazine *Aviation Week* sent staffman Clarence A Robinson Jr to Egypt to cover Exercise Bright Star. While there he was given a ride in a US, and the following is his story, reprinted with permission:

**Fayid Air Base, Egypt**—Aerial combat characteristics of the Egyptian air force Soviet-built MiG-21 Fishbed fighter were demonstrated here to AVIATION WEEK & SPACE TECHNOLOGY during a flight over the Suez Canal, Great Bitter Lake and the Sinai Desert.

The agility and handling qualities of the MiG-21, especially its stability at low speed, were displayed in a variety of aerial maneuvers by Brig Gen Nabil Farid Shoukry, chief of fighter operations training branch, flying in the front seat of the MiG-21US two-place aircraft, also called the Mongol. I occupied the rear seat.

**Aircraft Shortcomings**

Shortcomings such as the lack of an effective weapons system, limited internal fuel capacity and absence of a navigation system were apparent during the flight, which lasted approximately 30 min. The aerial maneuvering portion of the flight took place for approximately 18 min with numerous throttle excursions and afterburner lights.

Several thousand MiG-21s have been produced in the Soviet Union, Czechoslovakia and India with improvements in airframe design, avionics and the weapons control

ABOVE
*CL (Czech AF) No 1117 is an early MiG-21U with narrow fin, original braking-parachute location and no periscope, but it has a ciné camera on the right outboard pylon mount (P E Nordin via Robert J Ruffle)*

LEFT
*Close-up of the instructor's periscope in CL (Czech AF) MiG-21US No 0133. The aircraft has two pylons but the broad fin*

and weapon systems advancing later models of the fighter to an all-weather capability. This includes the advanced Atoll air-to-air missile with radar homing as well as infrared guidance.

A wing of Egyptian MiG-21 fighters operates from this base near the Great Bitter Lake and Suez Canal to control aerial approaches from the east.

Concentric air defense missile units are deployed in the desert surrounding the airfield.

All vehicles, aircraft and maintenance facilities are underground in hardened shelters of reinforced concrete covered by the desert sand.

From the air, only empty runways are visible.

When MiG-21s are launched on missions, the engines are started in the shelters and the pilots taxi directly into position on the runway, pausing only briefly before starting their takeoff roll.

This air base was captured by Israel in the October 1973 war, and hardened shelters were destroyed by demolition charges.

When Egypt regained the base and its land approaches across the Great Bitter Lake and canal, engineers rebuilt numerous aircraft shelters in the sand and covered them so they can withstand direct hits even from precision guided ordnance, officers here said.

There are far more shelters here than the 16-20 MiG-21 fighters in each of three squadrons. The aircraft frequently are moved from shelter to shelter in Egypt's own version of multiple protective structure basing using deception for survival.

The pre-flight inspection of the MiG-21 took place inside the aircraft's hardened shelter.

**Fuel Leak**

A large pan under the Mongol was used to collect fuel leaking from the internal fuel system. The aircraft can carry approximately 2,400 liters (634 gal) internally, and the Egyptian air force develops flight plans to permit landings with a minimum of about 500 liters (132 gal) as a safety measure.

After briefing me on how to close and lock the canopy and pressurize the cockpit, Shoukry, one of Egypt's leading fighter pilots, explained how to manually engage a gear tang on the throttle control system if it slipped out of synchronization while transitioning from the afterburner setting back to the military power setting. It cannot be engaged from the front cockpit, so if it slips it must be reengaged from the rear seat to avoid an in-flight engine emergency situation.

The ruggedness and simplicity in aircraft and avionics design was immediately apparent when getting into the cockpit. There is no navigation system in the MiG-21 aircraft, and instruments are at a minimum—a Mach meter, an altimeter, airspeed indicator, g-force meter and artificial horizon.

**Cockpit Features**

Radio switches on the right side of the cockpit are kept to a minimum. The throttle control is within easy reach at the left of the cockpit. The ejection system can be activated from the front seat or individually by pulling two D-ring type handles between the pilot's legs. The canopy and seat go simultaneously to form a kind of escape capsule.

The Tumansky engine was started inside the shelter, and within 3 min we taxied outside and moved quickly toward the runway.

Aircraft at this base are kept exposed on the ground for the shortest periods possible.

There was no other air activity taking place as we taxied into the takeoff position on one of three main parallel runways.

At opposite ends of the two outer main runways, runways jut off at obtuse angles. These runways are designed so that an attack down the main runways will still leave other runways from which operations can be conducted.

The flight control tower is a small mobile unit that can be positioned wherever required on the base.

In continual training exercises here, MiG-21s operating in the highest alert condition can be out of the hardened shelters and airborne for an intercept within 2 min 40 sec.

That is an average time for most wing pilots, not the fastest time, according to officers here.

Shoukry ran the engine up to approximately 80% power at the end of the runway in preparation for a maximum performance takeoff in afterburner, moved to 100% power setting and engaged the afterburner.

The Mongol trainer accelerated to the 700-meter (2,297 ft) point on the runway and was airborne.

Climbing at a 40-deg angle, the MiG-21 reached an altitude of 1,500 meters (4,950 ft) in 20 sec.

It can climb at a rate of 21,000 fpm at sea level, and at a rate of 10,000 fpm at 36,000 ft.

Shoukry's flight plan called for a heading directly east over the Great Bitter Lake, where we entered a sustained 6G turn to the left. The instruments indicated no loss in speed during the manoeuver, holding steady at an indicated 900 km/hr (493 kt).

The MiG-21 has a sustained turning rate of 7.5 deg/sec at Mach 0.9 at an altitude of 15,000 ft; an instantaneous turn rate of 13.4 deg/sec at Mach 0.9 at 15,000 ft, and 11.1 deg/sec at Mach 0.5 at the same altitude.

The afterburner was again engaged, and we began a zoom climb to an altitude of 8,000 meters (26,400 ft) at a rate of 450 fps, accomplishing an aileron roll as we climbed.

The Fishbed's heading was changed to the north, and we entered the air space over the Suez Canal and again turned to an eastward heading over the Sinai area where Shoukry flew split-S maneuvers before diving to an altitude of 800 meters (2,640 ft) heading due west to pass over the air base.

We descended to an altitude of approximately 150 meters (495 ft) and flew a slow roll over the runway at Fayid. The airspeed during the roll was 800 km/hr (431.2 kt).

The maximum speed for the aircraft at sea level, according to Egyptian air force officers, is Mach 1.06, and at altitude Mach 2.02.

The specific power for the MiG-21 at a 15,000-ft altitude at Mach 0.9 is 450 fps pulling 1 G; it is 50 fps pulling 5 G. The aircraft's thrust-to-weight ratio is 0.8, which compares with 0.63 for the Northrop F-5E, 0.72 for the Grumman F-14A, 1.08 for the McDonnell Douglas F-15, and 1.01 for the General Dynamics F-16A.

UPPER RIGHT
*Indian Air Force No U655 is a Type 66-600, with mainly early features apart from the broad vertical tail and relocated braking parachute (Robert J Ruffle archives)*

RIGHT
*The same aircraft is seen here on maintenance, with both KM-1 seats being removed. Note lack of outboard pylons and no AOA vane on side of nose*

## Performance Cited

Shoukry, who has approximately 3,000 hr in fighters and about 1,000 hr in the MiG-21, believes the aircraft's performance exceeds that of most fighters. He demonstrated the stability and handling qualities of the Fishbed as the flight profile took us back over the lake and Sinai areas.

The afterburner was engaged, and the aircraft responded by accelerating rapidly from 700 km/hr (377 kt) to 1,000 km/hr (539 kt) as a climb to 900 meters (2,970 ft) was accomplished.

Another 6 G turn was initiated and held for 360 deg before entering a climbing aileron roll with the fighter held at an intermediate power setting so that speed could be bled off to demonstrate the low speed and no speed handling capability of the MiG-21.

An indicated airspeed of 280 km/hr (151 kt) was reached and the aircraft remained fully maneuverable. As airspeed continued to drop, the maneuverability was sustained. With the stick fully aft, the aircraft turns easy.

The construction of the Fishbed is crude, but it is obvious that the aircraft was designed for rapid mass production. As an example, the boost assistance for the hydraulic control system makes it almost impossible for the pilot to overstress the aircraft in either angle of attack at G force.

The stick is stiff enough to prevent overstressing the fighter. The pilot must provide most of the force to the control surfaces.

## Stability Demonstrated

The aircraft demonstrated stability throughout the flight envelope, but visibility is limited from the cockpit both forward and aft.

The canopy has a thick design with bulletproof windscreen and offers limited visibility.

On the ground, a periscope in the rear cockpit gives the pilot in the second seat sufficient forward visibility to take off. As the landing gear is raised, the periscope retracts into a stowed position above the instrument panel. When the gear is lowered for landing, the periscope drops into place again.

Another climbing aileron roll and sharp turn to the right completed the planned maneuvering demonstration and Shoukry turned to a heading for the landing pattern. As the aircraft touched down, the fuel gauge indicated that approximately 900 liters (237 gal) remained.

The aircraft is solid on landing and exhibits a good shock absorber system. Again, a rapid taxi was accomplished to move from the runway to the taxiway and into the aircraft shelter as quickly as possible.

Shoukry explained after we reached the shelter that most of the wing pilots here fly approximately 20 sorties a month with the MiG-21 and that the wing is able to maintain a high operational readiness rate with the aircraft.

The general, who has flown the F-16 at Hill AFB, Utah, said MiG-21 squadrons are capable of flying approximately six sorties per day in each aircraft, but that after two or three days the unit must stand down for maintenance.

Egypt modified the MiG-21 in a variety of ways the Soviet Union later adopted and incorporated in later model export Fishbeds, according to Shoukry and Brig-Gen George Ezzat, the air force chief of repair and engineering. Ordnance points have been relocated and modified. The newer R-13-300 turbojet engine enables operation for 300 hr before an engine change is required.

This compares with 250 hr previously, Ezzat said.

The new engine also improves the range of the MiG-21, he said. When operating in afterburner, the aircraft is limited to approximately 15 min of flight time when maneuvering aerially so it cannot carry the external fuel tank on the underfuselage pylon, he added. Egypt has designed and produced larger fuel tanks for the fighter than the Soviet-built external tanks. They are produced at the Helwan Aircraft Factory.

The Model MF can fly for approximately 1.5 hr using the external tank configuration, Ezzat said.

Shoukry and Brig-Gen Mohammed Alaa Barakat, deputy chief of operations for the air force, said the real achievement is that the MiG-21s have been kept flying at a high operationally ready rate despite all the odds because of the lack of spares and support since the USSR was ordered out of Egypt.

This dictated developing an overhaul and maintenance capability in Egypt with support from Western nations.

## Chinese Aid

Some assistance has been received from the People's Republic of China, the two officers said.

Engines in the USSR for overhaul were later returned to Egypt after the Soviets left the country, officers here said. They estimate the number at 150 Tumanskys.

Both Shoukry and Barakat received their MiG training in the Soviet Union. Barakat is an instructor pilot with about 500 hr in the MiG-19 and 350 hr in the Sukhoi Su-7 ground attack aircraft.

The air base commander Brig-Gen Abdel Nasr, believes the MiG-21s in this wing compare favorably with any of the combat aircraft in the region, and that the combat experience and skill level of the pilots here make the aircraft difficult to defeat in aerial combat.

Major improvements are planned for the MiG-21, and a number of US companies are competing for contracts to upgrade the aircraft. Teledyne has a contract to develop and install an identification friend or foe system, which operates in the Soviet frequency range, making it compatible with other Soviet-built Egyptian equipment.

The company also is under contract with Litef, Litton's West German affiliate, to provide jointly a Doppler navigation computer and control display system for the German close air support version of the Dassault-Breguet/Dornier Alpha Jet. The system is integrated into the weapons delivery system with the head-up display.

Egypt wants a Doppler navigation system common to its air fleet and expresses strong interest in the Teledyne system for both fixed and rotary-wing aircraft, including the MiG-21.

The Egyptian air force operates with six combat versions of the MiG-21 Fishbed fighter, and a training version.

# Chapter 10
# The Chinese connection

Perhaps the strangest part of the whole MiG-21 story concerns China. Before the political break with the Soviet Union in 1960 the People's Republic had imported several MiG-21Fs. Back in January 1958 a licence arrangement had been worked out in respect of the MiG-19SF and its R-9BF-811 engine, but the severance of relations came before a licence arrangement for the MiG-21F had even been discussed. Despite this, the decision was taken to build the later aircraft in China as a matter of urgency, and according to Chinese statements the colossal task was done in four years. Bearing in mind the extreme shortage of technically qualified engineers, the total unfamiliarity with many of the devices and even the raw materials, and the language barrier, this seems almost beyond belief, and of course it involved the aircraft, engine and everything else.

Incidentally in 1969 Mikoyan emphasized to the author that his OKB had 'no knowledge of Chinese manufacture of the MiG-21'. Another Russian on a later occasion said 'It must have been like our work turning the B-29 into the Tupolev 4', doubly interesting because that is something most Russians never talk about.

The task of building the MiG-21F, under the PRC designation of J-7 (from Jianjiji = fighting aircraft), was assigned to the factory at Xian, which in pre-Pinyin spelling was Sian. The R-11-300 engine was designated WP-7 (from Wopen = turbojet) and assigned to the engine factory at Chengdu. This initial engine, as in the Soviet Union, was started on petrol (gasoline) drawn from a separate small tank, the pilot then switching to kerosene. The first J-7 was flown on 8 January 1965, and, remarkably, it is claimed the type entered service with the PLA (People's Liberation Army) air force in the same year.

In 1966, when over 60 J-7s had been delivered, the turmoil of the Cultural Revolution made continued manufacture impossible. As late as 1975 USAF Gen George S Brown said 'for reasons which are not yet fully clear . . . production was suspended and only a small number are operational . . .' The author has been assured that almost all the PRC aircraft programmes ground to a halt during this difficult period. Real production did not pick up again until after 1972, when small batches of the original J-7, restyled F-7 for export purposes, were delivered to Albania and Tanzania. Major production was resumed in the fifth Five-Year Plan (1976–80), incorporating numerous minor improvements aimed at curing specific faults and increasing troublefree life, and in particular, in doubling the 100-hour TBO of the original engine. The revised engine is the WP-7A.

By 1979 the senior engineers at both Xian and Chengdu had drawn up a schedule of much more extensive changes which involved almost complete reliance on Chinese designers. Some of these changes paralleled those already introduced in the Soviet Union, but in every case the modification was completely Chinese and in no sense a mere Chinese copy. Curiously the designation of the basic fighter remained J-7, but after 1984 the export designation was changed to F-7M Airguard to help the Chinese in their marketing at extremely competitive prices of about US $3.4 million in 1986.

The modifications were not introduced simultaneously, but all had been cleared for production by 1984. The engine went through two upgrades, the most extensive being the addition of a completely new and larger afterburner, with a better nozzle, in the WP-7B. In 1984 the WP-7B(BM) at last eliminated the starting tank, with an improved fuel system and burners able to start reliably on regular kerosene-type fuels. The inlet centrebody was improved in construction, made infinitely variable and placed under the control of an automatic electronic system fed by the pitots and yaw/pitch

ABOVE
*A rare flypast of J-7s during a military exercise in
northern China in October 1981
(Xinhua News Agency)*

*This J-7 cockpit shot gives a fine view of the canopy
arrangement and the CS-1 (Soviet = SK) ejection seat,
including the safety arm. Despite the fact that this
photo was taken in July 1985 the pilot is wearing an
early-pattern flying helmet instead of the standard
bonedome. A regiment of J-7s forms an impressive backdrop
(Xinhua News Agency)*

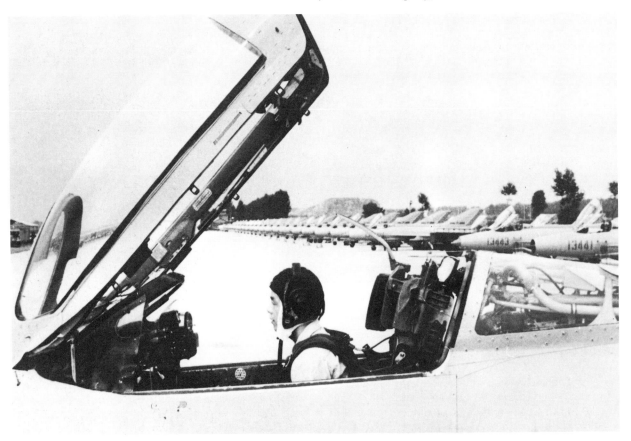

**ABOVE**
*Standing in front of a J-7, two Chinese fighter pilots describe a 1 v 1 air combat mission using models—a procedure repeated by fighter jocks everywhere. The leather flying gear may look quaint to Western eyes but its effectiveness in the bitter cold is undoubted (Xinthua News Agency)*

**RIGHT**
*Chinese copies of the K-13A AAM (already a copy of the AIM-9B Sidewinder) ready for fitting to copies of the MiG-21F!*

vanes on the air-data boom. The cockpit was made more modern in appearance, the seat replaced by a locally designed zero height/low speed seat of reduced weight using safety pins instead of an overhead arming lever, and the original canopy was replaced by a fixed bulletproof windscreen with a thin steel frame, plus an upward-hinged canopy giving more room and better view.

The dorsal spine was slightly redesigned, and at the rear faired into a new vertical tail of greater chord, with the braking parachute relocated in a cylindrical container at the base of the rudder. The left gun, removed from the original J-7, was restored, and ammunition feed improved (the gun has Chinese designation Type 30-1). Two additional outer-wing hardpoints were incorporated, with a choice of pylons for a much greater range of weapons, while the inner pylons were stressed for bombs of 500-kg (1,102-lb) size or tanks of 500-lit capacity (about 480 kg filled), giving the new option of an 800-lit centreline tank and two 500-lit wing tanks, whilst still carrying two

guns and two AAMs. The choice of AAMs was widened to include the PL-2 (K-13A copy), PL-2A (wide-angle SEAM Sidewinder copy), long-range PL-7 or French Matra R.550 Magic.

Inside the centrebody cone was installed a Type 226 ranging radar, probably (author's comment) derived from the Soviet R1L but offering many advantages including enhanced accuracy, a brighter picture and new ECCM qualities conferred by frequency-hopping and spread-spectrum techniques, making possible the guidance of the PL-7 semi-active homing missile. The Type 602 (Odd Rods) IFF was replaced by a new digital IFF of Western origin. The gunsight, invariably criticized even by the most dedicated MiG-21 drivers, has been replaced by a GEC Avionics Type 956 HUDWAC (head-up display and weapon-aiming computer), to which is also fed navigation information from a choice of navaids which in Chinese service still include the original radio compass and beacon receiver but in the F-7M offers a twin-gyro platform

LEFT

*The Shenyang J-6 (license-built MiG-19) has been
supplanted rather than replaced by the F-7 in the
interceptor role and is also used for attack and
reconnaissance missions. More than 3,000 are in service
with the Air Force of the People's Liberation Army,
compared to around 300 F-7s
(Xinhua News Agency)*

and strapdown inertial system. Other new avionics
include the GEC Avionics AD.3400 multifunction
UHF/VHF communications radio with secure
encryption unit, a digital air-data computer and Type
0101/HRA/2 radar altimeter from Smiths Industries.
The original electrical system was thrown out almost
in its entirety and replaced by a system with three
solid-state static inverters and improved wiring
looms.

The result is an extraordinary blend of old and
new, able to fly intensively in the harshest environ-

*Like most MiG-21s, the J-7 takes off without afterburner
to conserve fuel if enough runway is available*

ments and all at a price roughly one-third that of a
MiG-21 and one-fifth that of a fairly simple Western
fighter—and very much less than the best Western
advanced trainers. What really made the Airguard
possible was Saudi Arabian funding in 1981 for a
massive order for 160, split equally between Egypt
and Iraq. The Egyptian aircraft are supplied as CKD
(component knock-down) parts flown three at a time
in C-130s for assembly and flight test at the remote
Jiyanklis AB where a work force which in 1983 was
mainly Chinese bolted them together at the rate of
four a month. Indeed, part of the deal was that the
first flights would be made by Chinese pilots.
According to US reports the Iraqi F-7Ms were also
assembled at Jiyanklis, for collection by Iraqi pilots
and ferrying across Saudi Arabia and up the Arabian
Gulf.

The latest announced customer is Zimbabwe,
which after long negotiations purchased 24 F-7Ms
for delivery in 1985–86. Zimbabwe has no suitable
airlift transports and no indigenous aircraft assembly
capability, and it is possible these Airguards have
been shipped through Tanzania. According to
Chinese reports the F-7M carrying three 500-lit
tanks and two AAMs can make a five-minute
interception at a radius of 650 km (404 miles), which
is roughly double the radius of the 21F-13;
alternatively it can fly a 40-min CAP with the same
allowance for combat. Radar performance is not
stated, but AAM homing head lock-on range is said
to be 5–7.8 km for PL-2, 8–10 km with PL-2A and
14.4 km (8.95 miles) for the PL-7. The Chinese 57-
mm rocket launchers have 18 tubes (two more than
the standard Soviet pattern) and another optional
weapon load is seven of the massive 90-mm rockets
with an effective (though hardly precision-aimed)
range of 8 km.

# Chapter 11
# Related prototypes

In the 1950s the MiG OKB produced a series of larger prototypes using the same swept and tailed-delta aerodynamics as in the smaller Ye-2, 4, 5 and 6. These aircraft were of approximately twice the gross weight of their smaller brethren, and some had two MiG-21 engines. Most were in head-on competition with the reopened Sukhoi OKB for a production all-weather interceptor for the IA-PVO air-defence force.

First to fly was the I-1 (fighter 1), with OKB number of I-370, in November 1956. This had a 60° swept wing and Klimov VK-3 single-shaft bypass turbojet (low-ratio turbofan) of 8400 kg thrust. Compared with the contemporary Ye-2 it was not only bigger but the wing was mounted rather higher, the main gears had levered-suspension legs and there were many other differences, though the canopy/seat arrangement was identical.

Only a few weeks later came the I-3U (I-380), with small added wing-root sections housing NR-30 guns and with a kinked trailing edge. There were many other small changes, but this big fighter/bomber lost to Sukhoi's S-22, which became the VVS's Su-7, and the closely related I-3P interceptor also lost to Sukhoi's T-40 series which became the Su-9. In January 1957 the very impressive I-7K flew with the Lyul'ka AL-7F engine of 9300 kg thrust, reaching the remarkable speed of 2500 km/h or Mach 2.35. Via the I-7D, P and U the MiG team progressed by late 1957 to the I-75F, with a slightly bigger airframe with more pronounced area-ruling. This was fitted with a prototype of the Uragan (hurricane) radar, and with wing pylons for K-8 and K-9 missiles, the latter being the predecessor of the 'Anab' missile carried by the Yak-28P and Su-15/21. Unique features of the nose included a complete ring of auxiliary inlets and absence of an instrumentation boom.

Accepting defeat with the big swept-wing interceptors the OKB switched to the lower drag of the tailed delta and in 1958 flew the Ye-150, with scaled-up Ye-6 aerodynamics. The fuselage had to be redesigned to pick up the wing spars much further aft, and another change was the installation of the new Tumanskii R-15 rated at 9500 kg. This machine had no guns, and without the K-8 or K-9 missiles could reach the unprecedented speed for a fighter of 2900 km/h or Mach 2.73—distinctly faster than the prototype Phantom II which was parallel in timing.

From the Ye-150 was developed the Ye-152 with 10,220-kg R-15A engine, many minor airframe changes and a completely new integrated navigation and interception system with an advanced radar and weapon-aiming subsystem. The usual armament comprised two K-8 missiles, because all these aircraft came squarely into the time-frame in which guns were considered to be outmoded. The Ye-152 first flew in 1959, and towards the end of the year was joined by the first of 13 different but related MiG deltas to have twin engines. Designated Ye-152A, this machine had a fuselage redesigned internally to pass the air inlet ducts along the outer sides leading to two R-11F engines as then used in the series MiG-21F. The first 152A, with number 152 painted on it, was demonstrated publicly at Tushino on Aviation Day (9 July) 1961, carrying its K-8 missiles. The Ye-152Ms were prototypes of the planned series version, which was never ordered.

The MiG OKB achieved no VVS acceptance with any of these exceedingly fast aircraft, but what neither they nor anyone else expected was that 20 years later a derived aircraft would turn up in China! It is extremely doubtful that plans of the Ye-152A were given to the Chinese in 1959 in advance of a full licence agreement, so one must conclude that what the Chinese call the J-8, or F-8 in export form, is completely designed as well as built in China. The factory involved was Shenyang, and the J-8 has only a superficial resemblance to the Ye-152A, having a

*Despite its bulk and 25,088-lb (11,380-kg) weight, the I-75F achieved Mach 2.17 (1,430 mph, 2300 km/h). Note the K-9 missiles, an ancestor of the production 'Anab'*

ABOVE
*Parked in the open at the VVS Monino museum the 2681-km/h Ye-166 still looks awesome, especially to any pilot familiar with fast jets*

bigger wing and even more grotesquely tube-like fuselage. The length of 19 m quoted is actually slightly less than that of the 152A (19.8), but the latter figure includes the long instrument boom. Bearing in mind that the Chinese fighter has an F-7M nosecone instead of a large Uragan radar cone, the actual stretch in body length is in the order of 2 m (80 in). It is believed that only about 50 J-8s were built, most having the rear-hinged canopy of the F-7M (early

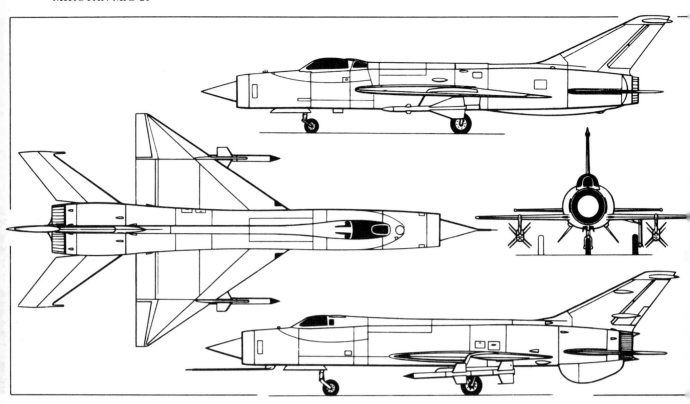

examples had the MiG-21F canopy as used on the J-7). Engines are WP-7Bs, again as used in the F-7M. Twin canted ventral fins are fitted, much longer than the deep curved ventrals of the Ye-152A. Lacking radar, the J-8 is a day fighter/bomber with two Type 30–1 guns in the fuselage and five pylons. In recent years the PRC has been talking with various Western companies about the possibility of upgrading this aircraft, in particular by fitting a modern multimode radar and medium-range missiles.

Arkhip Lyul'ka, whose smoky AL-7F-1 powered all the MiG Ye-23 series swing-wing prototypes and pre-series aircraft as well as the production MiG-23 (the initial sub-type without suffix), was in 1958 ordered to produce a special high-augmentation AL-7 for 'racing' purposes, which included setting speed records, conducting aerodynamic research and carrying out system and material tests at high speeds. The main reason was the need to build an interceptor to shoot down the B-70, the result being the Ye-266 and production MiG-25, and this required a back-up research aircraft. This also was assigned to the MiG OKB, and its design had to proceed with great urgency. The engine first flew in the Ye-152M, and as much of this existing 152-family design was retained as possible, to save time.

The new aircraft was designated Ye-166, and its outstanding feature was the totally new fuselage, with the modified 152M wings mounted almost exactly at the mid level. Predictably the aircraft was designed around the propulsion system, from the Oswatitsch nosecone, with four distinct cone angles, to the giant multi-petal nozzle. The inlet duct bifurcated immediately past the forward-placed cockpit with a tiny transparent hood. Downstream was a large spine leading to the new vertical tail, with forward-facing camera, and an equally new form of ventral fin. Fuel was put in every nook and cranny, but even so the fuel consumption in full afterburner was so great that no record could be attempted beyond 100 km. This particular circuit record was set on 7 October 1961 by A Fyedotov at 2401 km/h, the engine being coyly described to the FAI as a 'TRD Type P.166'. Thrust was said to be 10,000 kg, but in fact it was considerably greater. Next record to go was the world speed record over a 15/25-km course, set by Mossolov on 7 July 1962 in the Ye-166A with the fully-rated engine at 2681 km/h. The third and final record was a sustained height over the 15/25-km course of 22,670 m, by Piotr Ostapyenko on 11 September 1962. The records are inscribed on the Ye-166A which is preserved at the VVS Museum at Monino.

The Ye-230 STOL aircraft demonstrated at Domodyedovo on Aviation Day in 1967 was a member of the Ye-23 family, which led to today's MiG-23 and 27. It did, however, have a delta wing almost identical to several of the Ye-150 series, though with increased-chord ailerons and reduced-chord flaps. This hybrid had an AL-7F-1 engine, the same lift-jet installation as today's Yak-38 and semicircular lateral inlets like those of the F-104 or Mirage, alien to the MiG OKB.

Chronologically, the last of the prototype or

*The ultimate fighter prototype derived from the Ye-6 was the twin-engined Ye-152A, which had hardly anything in common with its starting point. The missiles were believed to be K-9s, and were given the NATO name Awl. Upper side-view is I-75F*
*(Pilot Press)*

*There are at least two different sub-types of Chinese J-8 twin-engined fighter. This is one of the earlier series, with MiG-21PF style canopy*

*This unusual view of the first prototype Tupolev Tu-144 SST, which had no retractable foreplanes, shows the shape of the wing originally flown in 1968 and backed up by research with the Mikoyan A-144* Analog *(next page)*

research aircraft related to the MiG-21 was the A-144. When in 1963 the GVF (civil air fleet) agreed on a go-ahead for an SST (supersonic transport) it was decided that the chosen tailless ogival delta configuration (the same as for the Anglo-French Concorde) should first be flown in small-scale on a supersonic research aircraft. After studying the prospects for building a completely new aircraft for this purpose it was decided to modify a MiG-21 of the latest MF series. Mikoyan set the first flight for early 1966, and assigned I V Frumkin as chief engineer on what was designated A-144, because it was to be the analogue of the Tu-144.

It proved to be about three times as big a job as had been anticipated. Though TsAGI underpinned the Tu-144 programme aerodynamically, the A-144 was supposed merely to be a MiG-21MF with an exact scale of the Tu-144 wing. Test pilot Oleg V Gudkov was assigned to the programme, assisted by col-

leagues Shchyerbakov, Fyedotov and Ostapyenko, and by 1964 they were getting to grips with the A-144 on a simulator at the MiG OKB. Enduring problems emerged with the dynamics of the aircraft, especially near the limits of the flight envelope which had to be explored even though no commercial SST would be expected to approach such extreme regions. More serious were the deep-rooted structural problems, involving inserting four massive spar frames into the tightly packed MF fuselage, evenly spaced from the front of the main-wheel bay (into which this particular frame protruded) and the tail. First flight came almost two years later than planned, by which time the first Tu-144, SSSR-68001, was complete and painted and undergoing ground testing. Mikoyan lived in the same block of flats (apartments) as Andrei N Tupolev, only one floor higher. Tupolev delighted to embarrass him by going up to the corridor outside the Mikoyan apartment and crying,

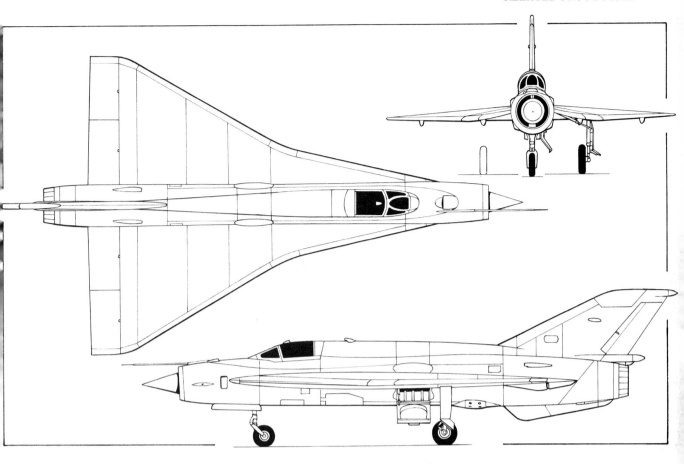

*Dwarfed by the No 6 pre-production Tu-144, SSSR-77106, the A-144 still rests honourably at the Monino Museum, showing several features (such as the spine bulge, nozzle surround and fin-tip pod) absent when last seen previously*
*(Klaus Niska)*

*This three-view shows the A-144 in its original configuration. Its wing was a close approximation to that of the original prototype Tu-144*

in a special plaintive voice, 'Artyem Ivanovich, *when am I going to get my Analog?*' Occasionally they would meet by chance in the lift, when Tupolev might just whisper the word 'When?'

Suffice to report the A-144 did fly well before the Tu-144, and proved that not a lot needed to be done to the SST's aerodynamics and elevon control system. It served as chase plane on the Tu-144s first flight on 31 December 1968.

# Appendices

## Appendix 1: Engines

The KB (construction, ie design, bureau) responsible for virtually all MiG-21 engines was founded by the dean of Soviet engine designers, A A Mikulin. Starting in 1916, he ended World War 2 as one of the most politically powerful men in the aviation industry. His engine KB was enormous, but Mikulin never really got to grips with gas turbines, leaving this to his deputy, S K Tumanskii. First production turbojet was the giant AM-3 (RD-3) series, followed by the slim AM-9 designed for the Yak-25 and MiG-19 twin-engined fighters. In the immediate post-war years the Aviation Minister, Khrunichyev, incurred Stalin's displeasure. He was ordered to be 'investigated', and Mikulin served on the investigating committee. For personal reasons he produced large amounts of evidence which incriminated Khrunichyev, who was arrested and expected imminent execution. Then in February 1953 Stalin died, and Mikulin's evidence was looked at more closely. Khrunichyev was quickly set free, and he lost no time in getting Mikulin dismissed and forced to retire in disgrace from public life. Tumanskii took over the KB, and from 1956 was designated official General Constructor, the 'AM' engines being redesignated with RD (reaction engine) numbers.

In 1952 Tumanskii designed one of the first two-spool engines, and in 1956 this became the RD-11, later simply called R-11. It was the first modern axial engine with an overhung first compressor stage and no inlet guide vanes. Thanks to the use of transonic blading the three-stage LP compressor achieved a pressure ratio per stage of 1.4; the HP compressor also had only three stages. Other features included a can-annular combustion chamber with ten flame tubes, two having igniters, two single-stage turbines, and a complex group of accessories on the underside (on the RD-9s in the MiG-19 accessories had been on top). A bit of added complexity was due to the use of a separate gasoline tank for starting, switching to the

main kerosene tanks taking place several seconds later when the engine had run up to full idling speed with adequate fuel pressure for kerosene vaporization. Gaseous oxygen injection increased maximum relight altitude from 8 km to 11.9 km.

The R-11 was not ready for early prototypes in the MiG-21 family, and these used the specially uprated RD-9Ye, inspected after each flight. The R-11S was first used in the Ye-2A and Ye-5 in 1956, rated at 3900 kg dry and up to 5100 kg with the afterburner at full power. The afterburner was particularly good for the mid-1950s, offering smooth lightup, full modulation and an efficient multi-flap nozzle. By 1958 the R-11F had been cleared for series production as the engine of the MiG-21F. Increased rpm and higher temperature raised thrust to 4300 kg dry and 5750 with full afterburner. In 1959 the F2-300 series introduced a larger afterburner which raised thrust to 5950 kg, and five years later this was raised to 6200 kg without reducing engine life. The FS-300 and uprated F2S-300 were developed specifically for later MiG-21s with SPS (blown flaps), with a manifold supplying the required large bleed flow left/right.

In China the original R-11F was refined into the Wopen 7B, rated at 6100 kg, and the WP-7BM in which the starting tank was eliminated and the combustion chamber and fuel system cleared for starting on fuel from the main tanks.

In 1965 the R-11 series was replaced in production by the R-13. This was deliberately made installationally interchangeable in the MiG-21 with its predecessor. The compressor was redesigned with higher work per stage and greater airflow, and the HP spool was given five stages, giving a substantial increase in ratings to 4250 kg dry and 6600 kg with maximum afterburner. These advances were accompanied by almost unchanged fuel consumption, such was the greater efficiency of the compressor and afterburner, while use of titanium instead of steel in

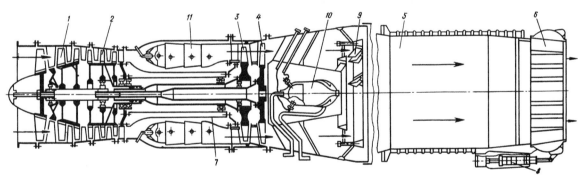

many large components reduced engine weight.

In 1970 the same process, taken much further, resulted in clearance for production of the final MiG-21 engine, the R-25. A completely new design, this was again installationally interchangeable, though it had rearranged accessories and is started with main aircraft fuel. Fuel consumption was again held at about the original level despite a further very large increase in ratings, to 6850 kg dry and 8000 kg (widely reported as 9000) with maximum afterburner. Overall pressure ratio of 14.2 is almost double that of the original R-11, and a major advance is the quite new two-stage afterburner which is claimed to be smoothly usable up to the highest altitudes reached

TOP

*This Tumanskii R-11F2S-300 was one of several hundred built under licence by Hindustan Aeronautics. The mass of ancillaries underneath includes a petrol (gasoline) starting tank, DC starter/generator and gearbox-driven alternator. On the side of the combustion chamber is the SPS bleed port*

ABOVE

*A simplified section through an R-11 afterburning turbojet. 1, LP compressor; 2, HP compressor; 3, HP turbine; 4, LP turbine; 5, afterburner; 6, variable nozzle; 7, main frame; 8, nozzle actuator; 9, afterburner gutters; 10, afterburner vaporizer; 11, combustion chamber flame tube*

Compared with the R-11 family the R-25 is a very similar twin-spool engine, even to the extent of having igniters in the same pair of flame tubes, but it handles a greater airflow and has a much better two-stage afterburner suitable for high-altitude operation. The SPS bleed-air connector is directly below the rearmost suspension cable by the MiG-21 (the brochure repeats the figure of 18 km), giving the MiG-21bis much better air combat performance at all heights.

The R-11F2S-300, R-13-300 and R-25 have all been produced in quantity by HAL at Koraput. This is today a major source of spares for MiG-21 engines.

# Appendix 2: Avionics

Over a period of 30 years the avionic equipment fitted to MiG-21 versions has changed dramatically. The following schedule is broadly applicable to the later versions, such as the MF and bis, though many items have been on all production variants and the three types of radar are listed.

## Radar

All early aircraft in this series were fitted with the SRD-5M Kvant (Quantum), called High Fix by NATO. This provided range only. The initial airborne interception radars were the R1L and R2L, code named Sapphire in the precious stone series and dubbed Spin Scan by NATO because of their scanning geometry. They provide target detection and guidance, as well as an important beam-riding function for the early Alkali AAM (carried by MiG-21PFs) and AS-7 Kerry ground-attack missile. The radar fitted to current variants is known to NATO as Jay Bird. It cannot guide the AS-7 attack missile, but it does provide the target-illuminating function for the AA-2-2 Advanced Atoll semi-active radar homing missile, which cannot be carried by earlier MiG-21 models.

## IFF

The identification friend or foe installation is either the SRO-2M or the upgraded SRZO-2, the latter being universal on current aircraft. All use similar 'pipes of Pan' scaled rod aerials, giving rise to the NATO name Odd Rods.

## ATC transponder

Standard fit is the SOD-57M, whose functions include automatic response to secondary radars and a major enhancement of radar signature, which was found vital for the MiG-21 to be seen on friendly radars.

## VHF

The very high frequency radio is invariably the RSIU-5, which operates in the 100–150 MHz waveband and is carried by most Soviet fighters and tactical aircraft (though not PVO interceptors).

## Datalink

The ARL-5 is the standard automatic air-to-ground datalink, which is compatible with Soviet GCI (ground control of interception) systems.

## Radio compass

Standard instrument is the ARK-10, very widely used in Soviet aircraft of many kinds. It provides a crude DME (distance-measuring equipment) function, provided it has a suitable responding ground target station.

## Radar altimeter

Standard fit is the usual RV-UM, served by a horizontal dipole aerial under either or both wingtips.

## IR sight

Most late models are fitted with the SIV-52, which has forward-looking optics and a refrigerated sensor, and is more capable than the seeker head of the K-13A (Atoll) and related missiles.

## Gunsight

Standard optical sight, linked with the radar, the ASP-5ND is fitted in several slightly different forms. Aircraft with the added gyro sight function have pitch and yaw vanes on the nose pitot boom.

## Launch Computer

Normal box is the VRD-24, into which can be inserted data for all MiG-21 armament schemes.

## Autopilot

Most MiG-21s are fitted with the widely used KAP-2, a simple analog equipment providing auto-stabilization and automatic flight-control functions with q-feel limitation, though probably left inoperative on most missions.

## RWR

All current MiG-21s have a radar warning receiver in the S-3M series, with two receiver aerials covering the aft quadrants from the top of the fin and two identical aerials in the leading edge of the wing covering the forward quadrants. Early MiG-21s had the Sirena 2, giving a flashing light and audio warning only. All current aircraft have Sirena 3, giving a visual display showing in which azimuth quadrant the threat is to be found.

# Appendix 3: Armament

## Guns

Early variants were armed with from one to three NR-30 cannon. This large 30-mm weapon was designed by the KB of Nudel'man and Rikhter and entered service in 1954. It weighs 66 kg (145.5 lb) and fires a 410-g projectile at the rate of 850 or 1,000 spm with a muzzle velocity (HE) of 780 m/s. Magazine 60 rounds. Standard gun in all later versions is the GSh-23L. This twin-barrel gun has a calibre of 23 mm and fires ammunition weighing (HE/API) 200 g at a rate of 3,400 spm with a muzzle velocity of 717 m/s. The external GP-9 pack contains 200 rounds, and the scabbed-on installation has a fuselage tank housing 220 rounds.

## Missiles

The only guided missiles normally carried by the MiG-21 have been for air-to-air use. The earliest type was the K-5A (NATO AA-1 Alkali), a canard beam-rider constrained to fly along the centre of the pencil beam of the R2L (or R1L) radar. Launch weight 91 kg, range 8 km, several sub-types. Nearly all MiG-21s can fire the K-13 family copied from the US Sidewinder AIM-9B. The original IR-homing version K-13A (NATO AA-2 Atoll) has a launch weight of 70 kg, length of 2.8 m and effective range of up to 4 km. The semi-active radar guided version (NATO AA-2-2 Advanced Atoll) has a length increased to 3.2 m and range of up to over 6 km when the target is illuminated by the Jay Bird radar. MiG-21s without this radar cannot fire this missile. All variants can carry up to eight R-60 (NATO AA-8 Aphid) advanced dogfight missiles, on twin launchers. This has a length of 2.15 m, launch weight of 55 kg and effective range of about 7 km. There is also a longer radar-guided version compatible with Jay Bird radar with an increased range.

## Other stores

Various FAB (free-fall GP bombs) can be carried up to 500-kg (1,102-lb) in mass. So can a very wide range of fragmentation, chemical and other bombs, as well as PTK bomblets scattered from cluster dispensers and BETAB retarded rocket-boosted penetrators for use against concrete. Nuclear weapons have not been seen on MiG-21s. The mass-produced 57-mm rockets can be fired from the UV-16-57 and UV-32-57 launchers, and the S-24 heavy rocket of 240-mm calibre can be carried on single or twin pylon interfaces.

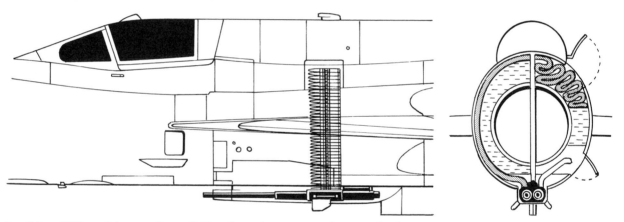

*In all late MiG-21 fighter versions a GSh-23L gun is scabbed on the underside of the fuselage between the nose gear and the centreline pylon. Normally fuel fills the space between the fuselage skin and engine air duct, But above the gun a dry bay is incorporated for the 23-mm ammunition. The cross section shows the doors for reloading (upper) and extraction of used cases (lower)*

# Appendix 4: MiG-21 operators

| Operator | Type | Quantity | Remarks |
| --- | --- | --- | --- |
| Afghanistan | MF | 70 | 3 squadrons replaced by MiG-23s |
| Albania | F-7 | 20 | |
| Algeria | F/MF | 70 | |
| Angola | MF | 85 | Cuban pilots |
| Bangladesh | MF/U | 9/2 | Delivered 1973 |
| Bulgaria | PF | 80 | 3 regiments |
| China | J-7 | 300 + | |

| Cuba | MF/PF/bis | 87 | |
|------|-----------|-----|---|
| Czechoslovakia | MF/R | 300/40 | 3 fighter-bomber regiments |
| East Germany | PF/MF/U/UM | 200/20 | Based Cottbus, Drewitz, and Marxwalde in 1st, 7th, and 8th fighter regiments |
| Egypt | F/PF/PFS/PFM/MF/U/US/F-7 | 100 | 60 F-7 |
| Ethiopia | PF | 100 | Cuban/East German pilots |
| Finland | bis/UM | 28/2 | No 31 Sqn, Kuopio-Rissala. Delivered 1978–80 |
| Hungary | F/PF/U | 100+ | 2 regiments/6 squadrons |
| India | F/MF/bis/U | 500 | MF/bis mostly built under licence. Total includes 40 Us |
| Indonesia | F | 20 | Retired |
| Iraq | PF/MF/U/F-7 | 90/6 | Armed with Magic AAMs |
| Laos | MF | 44 | 2 squadrons based at Wattay Airport, Vientiane. Delivered 1977 |
| Libya | MF | 94 | Some in storage |
| Madagascar | F/FL | 8 | 1 squadron |
| Mongolia | MF | 10 | Soviet-controlled |
| Mozambique | PFM/MF | 35 | Based at Beira but use Maputo Airport |
| Nigeria | MF/U | 31/2 | Based Kano |
| North Korea | PF | 120 | Being replaced by MiG-23s |
| North Yemen | PF | 25 | |
| Poland | PF/MF/RF/SMB | 385 | 35 RF |
| Romania | MF | 150 | |
| Somalia | MF | 10 | Poor serviceability |
| South Yemen | MF? | 50 | 3 squadrons |
| Soviet Union | PF/MF/RF/SMB/bis/U/UM | 1000+ | Mostly Frontal Aviation; rapidly being replaced by MiG-23 and MiG-29 |
| Sudan | PF | 20 | |
| Syria | PF/MF | 200 | Heavy attrition in Lebanese conflict made good by Soviet Union |
| Tanzania | F-7 | 15 | 4 lost |
| Uganda | MF | 10 | Status uncertain |
| United States | F/PF? | 6? | Used in Red Flag exercises. Acquired from Israel/Egypt |
| Vietnam | PF/MF | 150 | |
| Yugoslavia | F/PF/PFM/MF/U | 200/20 | Replaced F-86D/K Sabres |
| Zambia | MF | 16 | Delivered 1980, 2 lost |
| Zimbabwe | F-7 | 24 | Delivered 1986 |

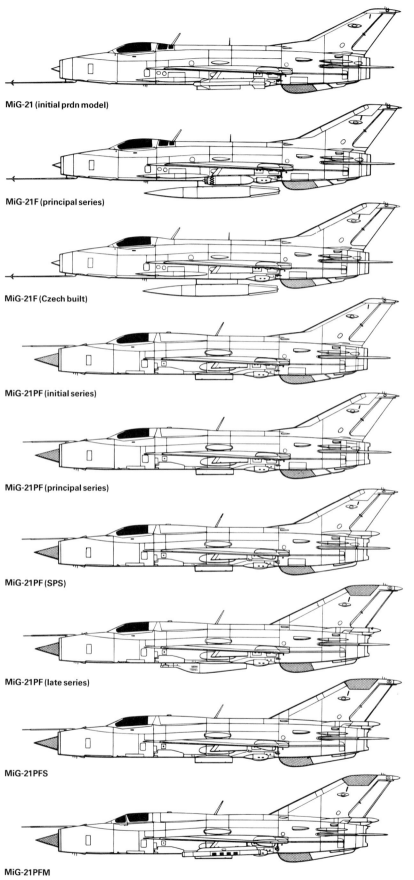

MiG-21 (initial prdn model)

MiG-21F (principal series)

MiG-21F (Czech built)

MiG-21PF (initial series)

MiG-21PF (principal series)

MiG-21PF (SPS)

MiG-21PF (late series)

MiG-21PFS

MiG-21PFM

## Appendix 5: Production variants and data tables

*These side view drawings can be studied in conjunction with the comprehensive data table overleaf, which gives approximate dates and other details for each version. Some of the modifications were introduced earlier or retroactively on other sub-types.*
*(mostly Pilot Press)*

*MiG-21: productionized Ye-6T*

*MiG-21F-13: extended-chord fin, slightly larger ventral fin, F-300 engine*

*MiG-21F (Czech-built): metal fairing behind canopy*

*MiG-21PF (FL similar): Sapphire radar, relocated nose boom, larger canopy fairing, gun(s) removed, modified forward airbrakes, 800-mm main tyres and thus larger bulges above and below wing root, F2-300 engine*

*MiG-21PF-13: extended-chord fin, extended upper and lower edges to tail end of fuselage*

*MiG-21PF-17: SPS blown flaps, braking parachute relocated at base of rudder, simpler ventral fin without cable channel*

*MiG-21PF-31: further extension to chord of fin, enlarged fairing projecting aft above rudder (but on this version, original flaps); shown with GP-9 gun pod*

*MiG-21PFS: PF-31 with SPS blown flaps and F2S-300 engine*

*MiG-21PFM: redesigned cockpit canopy hinged to right behind conventional fixed windscreen, KM-1 improved ejection seat (shown with ECM jammer pod)*

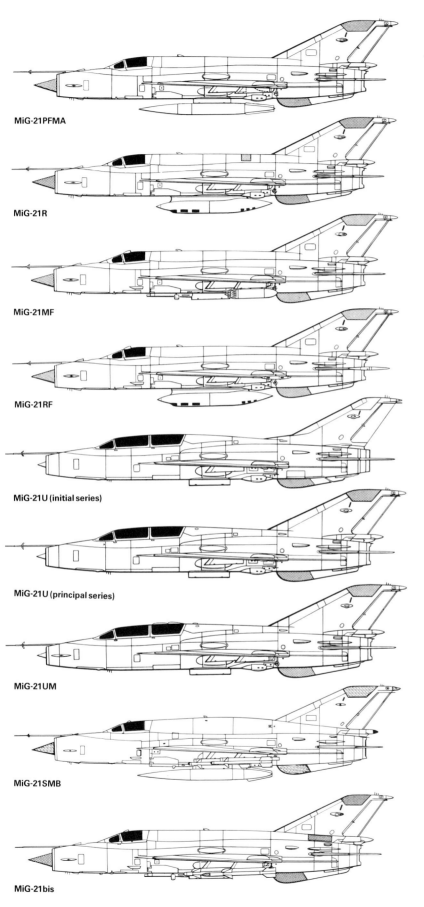

MiG-21PFMA

MiG-21R

MiG-21MF

MiG-21RF

MiG-21U (initial series)

MiG-21U (principal series)

MiG-21UM

MiG-21SMB

MiG-21bis

*MiG-21PFMA, or -21MA: enlarged dorsal spine, AOA vane on side of nose, four pylons*

*MiG-21R: provision for multisensor reconnaissance pod on centreline, extra radio navaid in spine under dielectric skin; provision for RWR aerials on wingtip pods (not shown)*

*MiG-21MF: R-13-300 engine, rearview mirror in canopy, internal' GSh-23L gun, anti-blast fences below auxiliary inlets*

*MiG-21RF: RWR aerials in wingtip pods, enlarged tailplane tip fairings*

*MiG-21SMB: R-25-300 engine, swollen dorsal spine extended across fin to meet braking-parachute compartment, RWR aerials in wingtip pods*

*MiG-21bis: definitive spine fairing, refined airframe, upgraded avionics for all-weather flight and controlled interceptions*

*MiG-21UTI/MiG-21U: derived from MiG-21F-13 with tandem cockpits, guns removed, revised tankage, single forward airbrake, 800-mm main tyres and enlarged mainwheel bay blisters*

*MiG-21U (suffix number unknown): extended-chord fin, enlarged fairing projecting aft above rudder, enlarged spine fairing, relocated braking parachute, extended upper and lower edges to tail end of fuselage*

*MiG-21UM: R-13-300 engine, AOA vane on side of nose, four underwing pylons. MiG-21US similar but R-11F2S-300 engine, SPS blown flaps, instructor periscope*

| OKB designation | | date (first ref.) | VVS designation | NATO designation | Engine type | static SL thrust (kg) | seats | canopy | internal fuel (lit) |
|---|---|---|---|---|---|---|---|---|---|
| Ye-2 | | 1954 | – | – | Tumanskii RD-9Ye | 3800 | 1 × SK | front | ? |
| Ye-2A | | 1956 | – | – | Tumanskii R-11S | 5100 | 1 × SK | front | 2120 |
| Ye-4 | | 1955 | – | – | Tumanskii RD-9Ye | 3800 | 1 × SK | front | ? |
| Ye-5 | | 1956 | MiG-21 | Fishbed | Tumanskii R-11S | 5100 | 1 × SK | front | 2350 |
| Ye-6 | | 1958 | MiG-21F | – | Tumanskii R-11S | 5100 | 1 × SK | front | 2340 |
| Ye-6T | (74) | 1959 | MiG-21F | Fishbed-C | Tumanskii R-11F-300 | 5750 | 1 × SK | front | 2470 |
| | | 1961 | MiG-21F-13 | Fishbed-E | Tumanskii R-11F-300 | 5750 | 1 × SK | front | 2470 |
| Ye-6U | | 1960 | MiG-21U | Mongol-A | Tumanskii R-11F-300 | 5750 | 2 × SKM | side (2) | 2400 |
| Ye-7 | (76) | 1960 | MiG-21PF | Fishbed-D/E | Tumanskii R-11F2-300 | 5950 | 1 × SK | front | 2850 |
| | (77) | 1963 | MiG-21FL | Fishbed-E | Tumanskii R-11F2-300 | 5950 | 1 × SK | front | 2776 |
| Ye-7SPS | | 1961 | MiG-21PFS | Fishbed-D | Tumanskii R-11F2S-300 | 6200 | 1 × SK | front | 2776 |
| | (92) | 1965 | MiG-21PFM | Fishbed-F | Tumanskii R-11F2S-300 | 6200 | 1 × KM-1 | side | 2776 |
| | (68) | 1964 | MiG-21US | Mongol-B | Tumanskii R-11F2S-300 | 6200 | 2 × KM-1 | side (2) | 2400 |
| | (69) | 1965 | MiG-21UM | Mongol B | Tumanskii R-13-300 | 6600 | 2 × KM-1 | side (2) | 2400 |
| Ye-8 | | 1962 | MiG-21I | – | ? | ? | ? | ? | ? |
| | | 1962 | MiG-21Sht | – | probably R-11F2S-300 | ? | 1 × SK | front | ? |
| | (92) | 1966 | MiG-21DPD | Fishbed-G | R-11F2S-300 + 2 × ZM | 6200 + 2 × 3650 | 1 × KM-1 | side | ? |
| Ye-9 | (88) | 1967 | MiG-21M | Fishbed-J export | Tumanskii R-11F2S-300 | 6200 | I × KM-1 | side | 2700 |
| | (94) | 1967 | MiG-21R | Fishbed-J | Tumanskii R-11F2S-300 | 6200 | 1 × KM-1 | side | 2700 |
| | (96) | 1967 | MiG-21MF | Fishbed-J | Tumanskii R-13-300 | 6600 | 1 × KM-1 | side | 2762 |
| | (96) | 1966 | MiG-21RF | Fishbed-H | Tumanskii R-13-300 | 6600 | 1 × KM-1 | side | 3000 |
| | (75) | 1970 | MiG-21SMB | Fishbed-K | Tumanskii R-25-300 | 7600 | 1 × KM-1 | side | 3350 |
| | (76) | 1971 | MiG-21 bis | Fishbed-L | Tumanskii R-25-300 | 7600 | 1 × KM-1 | side | 3075 |
| | | 1973 | MiG-21 bis | Fishbed-N | Tumanskii R-25-300 | 7600 | 1 × KM-1 | side | 3075 |
| Ye-33 | | 1965 | – | – | Tumanskii R-11F-300 | 5750 | 2 × SKM | side (2) | 2400 |
| Ye-50 | | 1955 | – | – | RD-9Ye + S-155 | 3800 + 3000 | 1 × SK | front | ? |
| Ye-50A | | 1957 | – | – | R-11S + S-155 | 5100 + 3000 | 1 × SK | front | ? |
| Ye-60 | | 1958 | – | – | R-11F-300 + S-155 | 5750 + 3000 | 1 × SK | front | ? |
| Ye-66 | | 1959 | – | – | Tumanskii R-11F2S-300 | 5950 | 1 × SK | front | 2470 |
| Ye-66A | | 1959 | – | – | R-11F2S-300 + U-2 | 6200 + 3000 | 1 × SK | front | ? |
| Ye-66B | | 1964 | – | – | R-11F2S-300 + 2 × TTPD | 6200 + 2 × 2300 | 1 × SK | front | ? |
| Ye-76 | | 1966 | – | – | Tumanskii R-11F2S-300 | 6200 | 1 × KM-1 | side | 2850 |
| A-144 | | 1968 | – | – | Tumanskii R-13-300 | 6600 | 1 × KM-1 | side | ? |
| F-7M | | 1982 | – | – | Wopen 7BM | 6100 | 1 × CS-1 | rear | 2470 |

| flaps | basic armament | radar | wing shape | empty | max T-O | maximum speed (km/h) and Mach | span | length (exc. probe) | wing area (m²) | remarks |
|---|---|---|---|---|---|---|---|---|---|---|
| slot | ? | none | swept | | c6000 | | 8.5 | c13.5 | 21.3 | |
| slot | 3 × NR-30 | none | swept | | 6250 | 1940 | 8.5 | | 21.3 | |
| slot | 2 × NR-30 | none | delta | | 6200 | | 7.4 | | c23.1 | |
| slot | 3 × NR-30 | none | delta | | 6250 | 2000 | 7.4 | | c23.1 | |
| slot | 2 × NR-30 | ? | delta | 4920 | 7650 | | 7.154 | | 23.0 | cropped tips |
| slot | 1 × NR-30, 2 × K-13A | High Fix | delta | 4980 | 8200 | 2125, 2.0 | 7.154 | 13.9 | 23.0 | |
| slot | 1 × NR-30, 2 × K-13A | High Fix | delta | 5000 | 8400 | 2125, 2.0 | 7.154 | 13.9 | 23.0 | extended fin |
| slot | none | none | delta | | | 2125, 2.0 | 7.154 | 14.41 | | |
| slot | 2 × K-13A or K-5A, GP-9 | R1L | delta | 5180 | 9300 | 2200 | 7.154 | 14.82 | 23.04 | |
| slot | GP-9, 2 × K-13A | R2L | delta | | | 2200 | 7.154 | 14.82 | 23.04 | relocated dragchute |
| blown | 2 × K-13A | R1L | delta | | | 2200 | 7.154 | 14.82 | 23.04 | |
| blown | 2 × K-13A or K-5A | R1L | delta | 5180 | 9290 | 2200 | 7.154 | 14.82 | 23.04 | |
| blown | none | none | delta | | 7640 | 2150, 2.02 | 7.154 | 14.41 | | |
| blown | none | none | delta | | | 2230, 2.1 | 7.154 | 14.41 | | |
| slot | heavy | ? | delta | | | | | | | |
| slot? | heavy | ? | delta | | 9500 + | | | 13.9 | | |
| blown | none | none | delta | | | 600 (limited) | ? | 16.0 | | |
| blown | GSh-23L, 4 × K-13 or K-5A | R2L | delta | 5600 | 9400 | 2200 | 7.154 | 14.82 | 23.04 | |
| blown | 2 × K-13A | R1L | delta | | 9590 | 2100 | 7.154 | | 23.04 | |
| blown | GSh-23L, 4 × K-13 | Jay Bird | delta | 5670 | 9800 | 2230, 2.1 | 7.154 | 14.82 | 23.04 | IR and radar K-13s |
| blown | 2 × K-13A | Jay Bird | delta | 5700 | 9800 | 2200 | 7.35 | 14.82 | 23.04 | span with RWR pods |
| blown | GSh-23L, 4 × K-13 | Jay Bird | delta | 5700 | 10,100 | 2250 | 7.154 | 14.82 | 23.04 | large saddle tank |
| blown | GSh-23L, 4 × K-13 | Jay Bird | delta | 5750 | 10,500 | 2200 | 7.154 | 14.82 | 23.04 | |
| blown | GSh-23L, 4 × K-13 or 8 × R-60 | Jay Bird | delta | 5750 | 10,500 | 2200 | 7.154 | 14.82 | 23.04 | improved avionics |
| blown | none | none | delta | | | 2.0 | 7.154 | 14.41 | 23.0 | |
| slot | 2 × NR-30 | none | swept | | | 2460, 2.31 | 8.5 | c13.5 | 21.3 | |
| slot | 2 × NR-30 | none | swept | | 8300 | 2600, | 8.5 | | 21.3? | |
| slot | ? | none | swept | | | 2600 + | 8.5 | | 21.3? | |
| slot | ? | none | delta | | | 2388, 2.247 | 7.154 | 13.9 | 23.0 | |
| slot | ? | none | delta | | | 2600 + ? | | 13.9 | | |
| slot | ? | none | delta | | | 2600 + ? | | | | |
| ? | no internal | R1L | delta | | | 2250 | | 14.82 | | |
| elevons | none | none | ogive | | | ? 2500 (E. Germ) | 7.8 | 14.82 | 27.2 | E. German span 11.5 (nonsense) |
| slot | 2 × 30-1, 4 AAM | T.226 | delta | 5145 | 8900 | 2175, 2.05 | 7.154 | 13.94 | 23.0 | |

# Index